10 Steps To Get Over An Ex...
For GOOD!"

By Devin Robinson X "Egypt"

Devin T. Robinson Copyright 2015

Table Of Contents:

Introduction
- What Should You Expect?

Section 1: Countdown To The 10 Steps

10: The Homeless Man You Know.
9: From Cheated On, Heartbroken to Heart Healer
8: Closure Is Imaginary. Take Blame & Win!
7: Why Should You Get Over Your Ex?
6: How Long Should It Take To Get Over An Ex?
5: Journey Is Different. Destination Is The Same
4: Till Death Do Us Part…Or.
3: When Will You Get Out Of Your Own Way?
2: Were They Worth Your Tears?
1: Do You Know You?

Section 2: The 10 Steps To Get Over An Ex…FOR GOOD

1: Stop All Communication.
2: Induce Thinking About Them.
3: Ban Sex/Intimacy With Them.
4: Remember…You Are An Ex!
5: Remind Yourself Why It Ended…
6: Realize You Are Broken.
7: Consult Guidance From An Elder or Mentor.
8: Have Fun!
9: Tomorrow Will Arrive.
10: Pray/Meditate.

- "The End"
- About Author
- Acknowledgments

Introduction:

What should you expect?

This book isn't meant to help those who actually want to be with their ex. This book isn't meant to make you feel guilty for cheating on your ex. This book isn't meant to coddle your emotions for being cheated on, betrayed or victimized by your ex. So...what should you expect?

Expect 10 Steps To Get Over Your Ex...FOR GOOD. With these 10 steps, you'll have an encouraging and comprehensive way to accomplish just that. Each step includes *Why You Should*, *Why It's Hard* and *Bad Advice Many Follow* which are important explanations needed to apply these steps properly. When you've concluded this book, you'll not only know these 10 steps, but you'll also learn about the steps needed before you're even ready to get over an ex. The pre-steps are called "Countdown To The 10 Steps." They're all part of a process endured by someone very similar to you...me.

As you will come to understand, I've been in your shoes...on both ends. Therefore, you'll notice I repeat myself often to drive home certain points I didn't listen to. My journey of being an ex covers much ground. I've been the violator and victim.

The violator is the person who cheats, lies, betrays or is at fault for the relationship's end. Enablers are included in the violator category. Why? When you allow someone to commit immoral acts, no matter how it ends, your hands are just as bloody as theirs. Why? You could have stopped the pain before it became unbearable. The victim is just that. Those innocent people who just didn't see it coming. You see, I've cried while being at fault and innocent.

Spending time on both sides helps me to empathize with your circumstances, not just sympathize with your hurt. Anyone with a heart and voice box can say, "You'll get over it." However, it takes someone who's been burnt by the fire of *starting over* to tell you, "Yes, you'll get over it. The "over" part won't be easy. Let me tell you why…"

Expect to be prepared, taught and encouraged. This helped me. I'm aiming to help you.

NOTES:

_____
_____
_____
_____
_____
_____
_____
_____
_____
_____
_____
_____
_____
_____
_____
_____
_____

**Choose You...
Smile Again**

www.GetOverThem.com

_10/_ The Homeless Man You Know

The inspiration behind this book.

Baby powder, baby wipes and baby oil. *Gifts from a previous relationship.* One black suit, one brown shirt, one pair of brown socks and one pair of black dress shoes. *Gifts from a generous thrift store.* One silver briefcase, 100 copies of his resume and three working pens. *Gifts from a former dream. These are his tools. This is his story.*

Daily, he goes to sleep with a goal. His mantra is, "One more 'No' to get a 'Yes'. Chasing a job from daylight until sun down. If not for the moon and exhaustion, he would grind himself to death. He needs to rest just to tag himself back into the rat race when he awakes.

During the hot summer months, his bed is under a bridge. Wearing only an under shirt, shorts and bare feet. His business attire is folded and laid under his briefcase. The briefcase's weight and summer humidity presses his suit. No matter the outlook of his circumstance, he still has dignity.

The shower in a free local gym keeps him clean. The baby powder and baby oil creates a healthy appearance. The scented baby wipes help prevent rashes and adds a pleasant smell to his body. Absence of daily meals gives the impression of fitness. With integrity, hope and tenacity, he searches for, "Now hiring," signs.

Once a well-known marketing expert in his hometown, now a homeless, jobless man in a foreign city. McDonald's, Wal-Mart and seemingly every fast food or supermarket said "No." They didn't know he was homeless because a P.O. Box and free government phone kept up a false reality. "Overqualified" was the reason. It was also rerouting.

Fear of rejection prevented him from applying for positions where being, "overqualified" would be met with adulation not denial. Another day without a meal and two more "No's" inspired him to take a chance. No more playing himself small, he aimed for bigger buildings and higher positions. His new mantra, "What more do I have to lose? No's don't hurt anymore."

Walking into the downtown business district going door to door has welcomed him with smiles and more "No's." The gold lined doors, elegant rugs and courteous executive assistants made the "No's" feel better. As the sun retired its job of brightening his path, he began trekking to the bridge. Head held high, with his spirits low, he knew things would change. Surrounding him were other homeless people watching his face as he entered the slums.

He is their hero. They pray for his victory. His extreme work ethic is noticeable by all. Many of them were once successful but drug addiction, the economy or just horrible unforeseen circumstances derailed their lives. Watching him try everyday gives them a reminder of their humanity. He donates a sense of hope for them. In return, they provide protection for him against some of the dangerous vagrants. The phrase used to comfort him is, "Tomorrow will be better." Tomorrow will.

Today only differs from tomorrow by the effort we exert. Now he's focused on staying downtown. Exerting more to get more. His baby face and thick hair gives the tidy image he needs to "fit in" the business crowd. Door to door he goes. "We'll keep your resume on file," "We're not hiring" and "Come back in the fall" are the new "No's." As the sun begins to fade, like tradition, he heads back to his unsheltered domicile. Walking into an elevator, he overhears a conversation between a man and woman about a marketing program for a new soda campaign. The ideas seem archaic to him. Without request, he interrupts the conversation.

He says, "Why show women in bikinis at a beach drinking soda? The world is more health conscious now. They'll drink water. Water is cheaper and actually quenches your thirst. Why not have them use it as a pick me up after a hard day at work right before being burnt out from the rat race? You should re-brand soda as an energy drink for busy people. Almost every busy person parties. It's already sold as a casual drink for partygoers. Give a different demographic better reason to buy your product. Inadvertently, the partygoers who are also busy will use this product as well. You'll hit two demographics for the price of one. On top of it all, most people consider themselves busy but fewer consider themselves partygoers. Anyway, have a great day." The elevator doors open, he exits and heads to the bridge. He's stopped.

A shoulder tap causes him to look back. It's the woman. She says, *"Hey, are you working for a company in this building?"* A slow disagreeing headshake answers her. She persists, *"Okay, are you working in the city?"* He replies, "I'm actually looking for a position." Reaching into his briefcase, "Here's my resume." She looks at it. *"You're work history ends three years ago. Where have you been working?"* He responds, "I've been looking for work." She says, *"For three years with this resume? You should have come to us once you left your last job. We're looking for upper level management. Someone to help redesign our marketing teams to adapt and compete with other top companies. Would you be interested?"* He smiles, as an unwanted but justified tear rolls down his face, he says, "When can I start?"

Entering the bridge area, his demeanor changes, the other nomads see his grin. They're aware of his impending good news. He discloses how it happened, how much he will make and when he will begin to work. They're excited, some cry and others begin to say how much they'll miss him. After a month of work, he leaves the bridge to live in an apartment inside the city. He doesn't forget the bridge.

He hires some of the homeless as janitors, consultants and employees; fitting them in where their talents and skills will better build the business. In seven years, he worked his way up to CEO. Many of the former homeless are now in management and creating opportunities for other people who lived under the bridge. One man's hope and determination changed many lives.

Why does this story matter to you? It's the reason why I wrote this book. My heart was broken and had no home. Poetically and figuratively speaking, my heart was homeless. The only tools I owned were faith and an image of, "I'm okay and happy." The clothes and smile I wore made this believable. Everyday I went out hoping to recover from the pain caused. I just wanted to be loved and love again. My "No's" came frequently.

I told many women "No" because they were unfit to love me. They were too similar to the exes who hurt me. Many women told me "No" because I was too similar to men who hurt them. Some "No's" came courtesy of me taking too long or lashing out with anger. From confusion, miscommunication, moving too fast, having sex too soon to being "too nice" or "too good to be true" were other reasons for "No's." Never was giving up on love an option.

Everyday I put on a suit of happiness and hope. It was "pressed" by my dedication to get over my exes and meet the woman God had for me. Other broken people surrounded me. Some handled heartbreak better than I. Some handled heartbreak worse. No matter how they dealt with heartbreak, they supported me. They protected me from women who would only damage me. They were my "homeless" community.

I found my wife by accident. She was a woman I spoke to briefly in Miami after I performed at her institution. Almost eight years later when I moved to Atlanta, she "tapped me on the shoulder" via an online message. After reconnecting, three years later we were married. After finding my "job"…my heart found a home. Shortly thereafter, I went back to the "bridge" to help others get "jobs" and help their hearts…find homes. *You are the others. This is my story.*

9/From Cheated On, Heartbroken to Heart Healer
The unexpected journey of becoming an author.

Have you ever seen two people who looked like they just…matched? When people saw my ex and I, they thought we were royalty. This was largely in part of our affinity toward wearing business attire and how our peers viewed us. We had arguments and happy moments but all and all, it was a beautiful adult relationship.

The day I planned to marry her was only a year away. She was "the one." I imagined a future with children, a house and happiness. As corny as it may read, I was "drunk in love." Forget butterflies, I was under the impression this woman was a Godsend.

She was like me in many ways. I loved her like I never thought I would love another woman. She came a couple years after my previous ex broke my heart by cheating on me. In my mind, heart and spirit, I knew this woman was different. She had to be…she was near perfect.

Six months before I was to propose, we began to have odd issues. Most of our relationship we were spoiled by being only a city away from one another. About two years into our love, she left for school. Long distance didn't hurt our relationship; the age-old, "lack of communication" did…well that's what I blamed it on.

Little by little, she stopped calling. We spoke less and less but argued more. Her excuse was "She's busy" yet I was the "busy" one. Her only duty was to be a student. At the time, I was a business owner, student, part of many clubs on campus and traveling the world as an author. How did she become busier than I? However I made sense of her actions, I permitted them. My *enabling* bit me on the butt.

One day, her phone was off, she didn't have any money and of course I wanted to speak to her on our irregular basis. Doing what I thought any loving boyfriend should; I paid her phone bill. During this time, we were arguing. She had been distant and we weren't having such lovely conversations.

Since she was always *busy* and we briefly spoke, I felt alone while in a relationship. Each day I would get two texts, a "Good morning" and "Good night". Maybe she would throw in a call or answer the phone. That was the totality of our interaction. To make matters worse, remember, we were in a long distance relationship. Communication is vital in long distance relationships. If you can't physically touch, the voice becomes a very important component of the union. Despite the aforementioned, I paid the bill anyway. As I logged into her account to pay, something broke my spirit in ways I wouldn't wish on any enemy.

During this time, there was such a thing as the "Fav Five." This is where you could add your five favorite people and talk to them unlimited. Searching through her account to find the pay button, I stumbled across her "Fav Five". Her "Favs" included, "My Boo", "My Boo's House", "Guy Best Friend", "Female Bestie" and "Devin Robinson." You're probably smiling at how special I must have felt. Three numbers just for her boyfriend. Here's the problem, I only had **one** phone number. Therefore, "My Boo" and "My Boo House"…weren't my numbers.

Deflated isn't half of what I felt. There is nothing like being a public figure traveling the world to inspire people about love, faithfulness and the beauty of companionship while being deceived by someone you loved. No words could describe my doubt in love at this time. How could this be love if it hurts so much? Of all people, she wasn't supposed to be the one to do this to me.

Remember, this was "the one." I was embarrassed because I've told friends, "I'm proposing in July." She met my family and I met hers. We planned a life together. There wasn't supposed to be an end. This woman was to receive my last name. Instead, I received pain.

Of course I called her to detail my discovery. She didn't hide anything and blamed me for pushing her to such an extent; something I still don't understand. Before I could feel my first tear fall…it was over. All that time. All that energy. All that "future" was gone.

Flash forward to Spring 2009; Kanye West released a legendary accumulation of messages that defined my heart's condition. The song was called, "See You In My Nightmares." Accompanying Kanye was rapper Lil' Wayne. When he delivered his rap (sermon, to be precise) it painted my agony in ways I couldn't describe.

"Baby girl I'm finished
I thought we were committed

> *I thought we were cemented*
> *I really thought we meant it*
> *But Now we just repenting*
> *And Now we just resenting"*
> *-Lil Wayne*

This song, although not relative for a happy person, was a release for my anger and defeat. The feeling of losing someone is unbearable and even worse when you have to face all of your loved ones who knew it wasn't going to last. After this song gave me an outlet for my frustration, something amazing happened.

I've been cheated on twice…in back to back relationships. Heart broken would be an upgrade to how I felt. Some days I burst into tears randomly. Crying at the confusion and pain caused. Sometimes, I would violently rant using disgusting language to describe my woes. What came out of that turmoil wasn't hate for those women…but a book to help those like me to get our minds back, love again and get over our exes…FOR GOOD!

8/ Closure Is Imaginary. Take Blame & Win!
It may make you feel good…but it's not what heals you.

One **DIFFICULT** thing you must do before reading the 10 steps is…take blame for what you did. I'm not implying you did something wrong because in many cases blame sits squarely on one party. However, blaming them isn't always a source of healthy power. What I'm encouraging is to find the part of your story where you had the power to change it.

My first ex cheated, yes, but I could have left earlier when her depression became too painful to bear. No, I don't take blame for her cheating. I take blame for not leaving sooner. I had the *power* to leave earlier; I had no power to stop her from cheating.

My second ex cheated, yes, but I could have left earlier when she continued to make me #48 on her priority list. No, I don't take blame for her cheating or prioritizing me last. I take blame for not leaving sooner. Especially after being treated so poorly and undeservingly. That's the power I had but <u>didn't use.</u>

Why take blame? You can control what you did. You can't control what they did. Until you own power over a situation, you'll be a slave to their apology, explanation or "I'll never do it again." None of which heals you; it just prolongs them being in your life and adds an unnecessary fact your mind has to deal with.

Many people lie to themselves by wanting, "closure." Closure is slavery of the mind and spirit. How? Even though you're given a reason, you will find a way to bond yourself to an old experience. If they say, "I left you *because*…" you'll find a way fix yourself or consider fixing yourself in order to satisfy their failings. The *"because"* will hold your heart hostage. Waiting for someone to disclose why they abused your trust, heart and future is pointless.

Both of my exes gave me, "closure." After they told me, the first move I made was figuring out how to get them back. I tried to fix the *"because."* I failed both times. Why? They're exes for a reason. The problem isn't just what they did but why they did it and who they are. The *why* and *who* are truly embedded in their character. Therefore, it's a *"because"* God has to fix…not me. Here's a story.

My father left my life a day or so after my mother died. Honestly, he wasn't really there before then. No matter the fact, he didn't wait until I was an adult or even a teenager. He just left a 12-year-old boy to figure out life, manhood and mourning without a father. Almost 20 years later, we spoke. I harbored this anger, hatred and BLAME for so long and couldn't wait to unleash it upon him. One discussion I asked, "Are you ever going to apologize?" He did what many exes do.

He said, "If you need an apology, I mean, yeah, I apologize but let the past be the past." That, to me, was the weakest, most insincere and unapologetic apology on earth. Yet, it was what I thought was needed to get me over the hump of being abandoned by him. I completely neglected all of my achievements gained without him in my life. His not being there may be the reason I'm as successful as I am. *Maybe if he would have been in my life, I wouldn't be as special as I am.* Funny thing, those last words…were his.

Honestly, nothing they say or do will fill the void, agony or injury they caused. You may think so, but it doesn't. It's not meant to. If you think they can intervene and make things better…think again. Your power lies in what you can control. You control your faith. You control how you respond. You control what, when and how you forgive.

They owe you nothing. Even if they gave it, you would still not believe their reasons, apologies or puppy dog eyes. In the back of your mind, they are tainted. Forever stained by their actions. If you were the reason it ceased, why reintroduce yourself to a relationship bloodied by the war that ended it? It's time for you to get over it and get over them.

Until you do…how can God heal you? Time heals all wounds but sometimes…time is a synonym for God. If you're too busy drowning in bad decisions, how can God give you air? That last line may appear cheesy, but really think about it.

A 12-year-old can't take blame for his father leaving him. No, that's unfair and impossible. What I could take blame for is the amount of time I wasted believing his apology would set me free. That a word or group of words would heal me. My power was in advancement. He had nothing to do with my success. He can't take part or a portion of credit in my journey. Those scars didn't hold me back. It was the imaginary hope that the same person who scarred me…would be the one to heal me.

Take blame for what you can control and then take control of your circumstances. You are bold, powerful and deserving of being loved. If you don't take the time to do the above, the baggage you hold will enter every relationship and wear down an innocent person who only wants to love you.

Even if you get closure, which is great and may take weight off your shoulders, understand it's not the defining factor in recovery. You hold the power of choice in your pain.

Before you continue, make a choice. Will you be in control or allow someone who is no longer obligated to love you…to dictate the future of your heart?

7/Why Should You Get Over Your Ex?
What we seldom ask while hurt.

Since April 6th, 2014, I've been married to the WOMAN OF MY DREAMS! She's brilliant, beautiful and BOLD! Without a doubt, when I dreamt of my ideal wife, this woman came to mind. Anything I could ever imagine in a mate is tied into this woman.

Her awkwardness makes me laugh. Her innocence makes me protective. Her happiness…makes me happy. On top of it, she knows how to love me.

She supports my vision. I support her vision. She's bought EVERY book I own and read them. I've helped her study for exams. (Something I would rather not do again…my gosh! All those 20 letter medical words still haunt me.) We teach each other new things. She encourages my upward mobility. I encourage her goals. She prays for and with me. I pray for and with her. She loves my family. My family loves her. Her mother and father both love me. Her mother is a supporter of my work. Despite how beautifully we are connected, something almost ended what became an inspiring relationship between two loving Christians.

My ex came back into my life. After the man she cheated on me with broke up with her, I was an easy target. She told me he broke her heart by saying, "I never loved you." Even with this revelation, she still had a round-trip ticket back to my heart.

She didn't come into my life without an invite. She was welcomed with open arms, a smile and hopefulness. This was a dark moment but I disguised it as a bright day.

Before my wife and I began dating exclusively, my ex was given my attention. *She didn't take my attention. I gave it away.* What suckered me in was the possibility of her being what I thought she was, not who I *knew* she was. Again, when it's a character issue, the change happens when God intervenes, not you.

As I slowly started to march towards a rekindled relationship with my ex…something stopped me. It was God. It had to be. I wasn't strong enough. I wasn't powerful enough to dodge returning to the person who inflicted an unbearable wound in my heart. For some reason, I took a break from both women by ceasing communication for a month.

This month was a blessing. My mind was clearing. My heart was unlocking the chains my ex re-laced across my heart. My vision began to see truth…she was not the one.

I followed all of the steps and got rid of my ex…for good. Amazingly, I wouldn't have been married to my wife if God didn't get this woman out of my system. Imagine, if you don't get over your ex, will your future husband or wife evade you? Will you ever find peace in solitude? Will you ever be happy? This is why you have to get over them. Not just for the love of someone else but the peace and happiness you owe yourself.

6/ How Long Should It Take To Get Over An Ex?
A complicated equation with a simple answer.

A wealthy and cocky young man was running through a 50-mile trail. Stumbling across a certain image slowed him down. There was an old homeless man wearing an offensive shirt. The shirt was only offensive to the young man and others like him.

The front read, "World's Greatest Runner", on the back, "Undefeated." Upset, he approached the old man. *"I've been running for 7 years. In that time, I amassed 4 national titles and 3 state records. No one is faster nor can run longer than I. How could someone 3 times my age with those dirty old shoes dare wear a shirt displaying such a bold and evidently false claim?"* The old man replied, "It's not false. I bet I can run longer than you, easily."

Amazed, the young man responds, *"What do you say, if I win, you give me the shirt?"* The old man nods in agreement and says, "If I win, you buy me some new shoes and a one night hotel stay?" The young man tops him and says, *"How about I give you two new pair of shoes and $100,000 for a house?"* With a smile and without a blink, the old man says, "Let's go, but on one condition. Since I'm old, I'll need some help." The young man said, *"Sure, you want a* *head start?"* The old man says, "No, just allow me to set when we're finished." The young man agrees.

They get to the starting line. "Go!" the young man yells. They run. The young man sprints off. Leaving the old man in the dust. There isn't even a challenge. The old man runs at a steady pace.

Noticing how far he's left the old man behind, he attempts to embarrass the old man. Showing off, the young man does jumping jacks and cart wheels while running. He even runs back to the old man just to ask, *"How long until we're done?"* The old man replies, "I'll tell you when." The young man runs full throttle ahead. Again, he leaves the man far behind him.

As time passes, the young man gets tired, runs back to the old man, he asks, *"Where's the finish line?"* the old man says, "I'll tell you." Exhausted, the young man keeps pace with the old man. As time progresses, the young man slows down and eventually collapses. The old man takes two steps ahead of the young man and says, "Where I'm standing is the finish line. I won."

What's the moral of the story? As long as someone other than you dictates when you've gotten over an ex, you'll always wait until they reveal the "finish line."

Honestly, the time is based on when you are truly ready to get over them. I genuinely believe you will never have them out of your system in the sense that they won't ever be thought of. That's impossible solely because when we use the words "I love you," we plan on loving that person forever.

We're taught that love isn't finite. You say, "I love you" and will do so until the person or you is dead. Therefore, you will always care and think about them. The difference in actually getting over them is when caring and thinking about them no longer affects you negatively or positively. To add, when you no longer want to be with them or care to engage in even a hypothetical conversation about revisiting a relationship with them, you've moved on.

After dating me, my exes have had children, entered multiple relationships and have done great things…but their success or failure has no bearings on my happiness. Sure, you can be happy for your ex but it shouldn't affect your relationship or personal state of joy. The, "I'm happy for you" is more of a sincere gesture than a declaration of how bright your day is now that your ex is married or divorced.

That's where loving again happens. Once you get to a place where nothing they do can make you revisit their love, attention or treatment, then you can love again. When you have no hope in a "What if" with your ex, that's getting over them. When you no longer want to know how they're doing or really are burdened or joyful if you do find out, that's getting over them.

To break it down in a formula, typically it should take half the time you were together to reach a point of, " *I'm ready to get over them."* It takes time just to get there. Being ready to get over someone is a journey in itself. Why? During this time, you're still going through 7 stages of grief and those aren't stages you get over quickly.

A breakup resembles losing a loved one because you actually are losing someone forever, at least emotionally.

Here are the stages you may go through:

Shock & Denial

This is when you realistically can't believe you two are over. You revisit pictures, thoughts and places where you two added to your relationship. This is the phase that seems to last forever because you honestly never thought this day would come. Even though you may have seen the writing on the wall, this phase still results in disbelief.

Pain & Guilt

Can't eat, sleep or go outside? That's the pain portion. In the same stage, you'll find yourself making excuses as to why you're to blame for the end. If you are to blame, you'll take more of the pain from losing someone who didn't deserve what you gave or someone you lost but didn't want to lose.

Anger & Bargaining

As you begin to conjure up all the reasons to hate them or yourself for allowing their actions or your actions, you bargain with yourself.

You will read and live the infamous and never ending novel, "What if."

At this time, you will replay the situation in your mind to figure out what you could have done to change the circumstances. As you realize no answer is possible since the relationship is over, your anger will grow. Fortunately most don't explode outward. They never really harm others with their feelings.

Unfortunately the inward explosion (implosion) causes for self hate, self-doubt or even suicidal thoughts to grow. It's at this level where many stay and create battle plans to inflict harm on their ex, new mate or even themself.

Depression/Reflection/Loneliness

It's at this point where you realize they are gone. When you realize what you two shared is no longer part of your future story, you may feel lonely. At times, you may even own the belief of brokenness. This is typically a result of believing a person completes you. That's false.

A person doesn't complete you. They add to you. It's not about two broken people creating a whole relationship. That's how more abuse and pain occurs. It's about two whole people entering and creating a relationship together.

The Upward Turn

After your friends got used to you previously declining any activity that required boosting your spirits, you then surprise them by suddenly asking for details on the next event. You can't stay sad forever so you actively look for things to do. Your spirits lift and you realize life without them isn't the end. It's just a new beginning to your story.

Reconstruction & Working Through

From here, you build on the new found happiness. You aren't ready to be in a relationship, but you can see yourself in one. You can actually smile at the idea of being in love. Reading books on love, relationship building or articles on do's and don'ts of love fill this point.

Acceptance/Hope

Now you're ready to love again. The person may still be in your mind time to time but you won't find yourself in bondage to their actions, whereabouts or contact. Although dating will be new, it won't be difficult.

You won't fall in love right away, but you'll make sure this next person isn't as flawed as the last. You'll be more conscious of avoiding the same mistakes you made in the previous relationship.

Learn more about the seven stages of grief at www.recover-from-grief.com

Once you've overcome these stages, you can begin to fully get over your ex and be ready to say, "I deserve to be loved again." From three to seven months is typically the time I've noticed is needed to get over an ex after the previous process.

The time varies based on the intensity of the relationship. Contributing factors to lessen or elongate the time are:

> 1. Having family/friends who encourage you to stay with the ex.
> 2. A mentor who directs your path during this moment or lack thereof.

3. Your attention to faith and/or consistency of prayer or lack thereof.

4. You habitually converse with your ex on an intimate level.

5. Being over 25 and feeling the heavy urge of marriage.

6. If you've already begun to leave them emotionally before you two broke up or if the breakup was sudden and unexpected.

There is no exact science of a timeline, which I've researched. In the end, it's based on how much time it takes you as an individual. I've seen people ready in six months. On the flip side, I've seen people still scarred by their exes for nine years. The finish line is based on you.

5/ Journey Is Different. Destination Is The Same.
I asked seven people three questions about getting over an ex.

Names have been altered to protect the privacy of participants.

1. D. Axantus

Delray Beach, Florida

Why did the relationship end?

"I ended the relationship because I saw no hope of the improvement of my ex-boyfriend's behavior. He had changed from a God-fearing promising student to a dope dealing class 1 moocher and abuser."

How long did it take you to get over them?

"It took me a length of about 2 years in which I returned to my ex about 4 times just to experience more disappointment and abuse."

What steps did you take to get over them?

"I started preparing for the breakup long before it even happened because I knew I deserved more. The hardest part is actually going through with the break up. I had run all my friends and even some family members out of my life with my relationship drama so I took on most of my healing alone.

I immersed myself in soul searching, researching, reading, meditation, exercising to blow off steam and tons of writing. As a woman whose self-esteem had been totally blown I had to dig deep within myself to salvage my self worth, love, motivations and passions in order to move on."

2. B. Anne.
Boca Raton, Florida

Why did the relationship end?

"Relationship ended after two and a half years. We were both 19. He started pushing away which led me to become very suspicious of his intentions. This also caused me to break up with him only to find out that he did want to end the relationship to go sleep around. Unfortunately he didn't have the courage to end it himself."

How long did it take you to get over them?

"It took me over a year to get over him. I was already in a relationship with someone four months after we broke up. I wanted to move on because he was my first; the only person I had ever been with. I wanted to change that."

What steps did you take to get over them?

"I started dating this amazingly kind man four months after we broke up. It was hard but I was very honest about my past relationship and he understood. We took things very slowly and he was very patient with me.

I prayed a lot for God to help me get over the break up because I didn't want to be bitter and angry towards men. And now four and a half years later, the kind man I met 4 months after my breakup is now my fiancé. We are planning our wedding soon!"

3. M. Worthington
Miami, Florida

Why did the relationship end?
"It was pretty bad. I met the brother at church but I found out he was a gold-digger, liar, cheater and although he occupied a great function at church, the brother wasn't even saved!"

How long did it take you to get over them?
"It took me 2 years to get over my last one."

What steps did you take to get over them?
"Mostly prayer helped and I had to learn to love myself, not only did I regain my confidence but also self-esteem to heal the wounds and pick up the broken pieces. Now, I'm so glad that it was earlier than later because no matter how excruciating the pain was, it could have been worse. Like they say, "what doesn't break you makes you stronger". Well I am no longer naïve. I've also raised my standards. Enough said; God is able."

4. V. Bibbetts

Minneapolis, Minnesota

Why did the relationship end?

"We were both really unhealthy people. I know we loved each other, but the relationship had been sick for some time and on and off like they go, and finally it was just the end. He left me."

How long did it take you to get over them?

"It came and went for a long time. It was a process! When we made amends to one another, I think that was the point where I would say I was at peace with it, so it took almost two years."

What steps did you take to get over them?"

I had a lot of help and support. I spent time with positive people who listened to me because I had to talk about it. And I talked about it a lot. I cried a lot. But I didn't let it break me. I let it empower me to move forward. I made good decisions for myself and put myself first. I talked to God a lot.

I really connected with my spirituality. I spent a lot of time outside looking at the sky or being by the water, praying and practicing my culture. I began living the life I was meant to, and in that, I felt good and got stronger.

I took care of myself. Exercise was and still is really important to me! It's meditative, feels good, is healthy and nurtures my body and mind. I remember I would have restless nights where my brain wouldn't shut off, so I would go for a run to feel better. It would calm me. There was a lot of pain, and there were different points where I felt stabbed by it. You know, seeing him with his new girlfriend and things like that. But I would take a deep breath and move forward.

There were also a lot of times where I wanted to talk to him or I wanted to just break down and tell him off, but I would turn away from that. Each time I made a good choice to move away from the past, I would get stronger and it became easier to make those choices. I gave myself the time to heal and believed that in time, I would heal like everyone told me. They were right, because I did! So it took a lot! But I am so glad I went through that. Everything went just as it was meant to, I believe."

5. D. Mannor

Pembroke Pines, Florida

Why did the relationship end?

"The relationship ended because she pushed me away & I was tired of the dysfunction. In our 2-year relationship, this was our 3rd breakup & I couldn't take the rollercoaster anymore.

She had unresolved issues from previous relationships & it manifested in her doing things to push me away but still stay within reach. I was unaware & it resulted in me developing insecurities myself. I couldn't deal anymore."

How long did it take you to get over them?

"It took about 3-4 years, but closer to 4."

What steps did you take to get over them?

"I had to sort thru the baggage I had accumulated. The 1st step was getting closure. After we had broken up, I was under the impression that everything had been because of me & my inadequacies. It wasn't until we had a conversation some 8 months later that she told me about the issues she'd been carrying & I realized the fault wasn't on my end. Step 2 was finding my role in the problems. Now that I knew what she was responsible for, I had to find what I was responsible for. I had removed God from the relationship and had carried on an affair behind her back. Things I'm not proud of.

Once I discovered those I was able to learn from them. My 3rd step was to kill my insecurities. That required me to relearn how to love myself by spending time with myself. I was still in the relationship I had behind her back, but I had to end that because it was still part of the baggage.

Remaining single and actively spending time by myself helped me figure out who I was again. The relationship & break up broke me. I'm different from who I was before I met her. The me today is stronger, wiser and more seasoned. My 4th step was to prepare for my next relationship. This is ongoing. I'm taking my time & allowing patience & discernment to do its thing, but I'm also building a castle for my queen. I'm working & saving, pursuing education, focusing on short and long-term goals so that I have the best to offer for my next & hopefully last relationship, as well as myself."

6. F. Benoit
Lakeland, Florida

Why did the relationship end?

"My ex is my kids' dad. Once he found out I was pregnant with our second child he left me and began dating someone else. He moved her into his parents' house with him and she may be pregnant also."

How long did it take you to get over them?

It took me six months to get over the whole situation."

What steps did you take to get over them?

"I prayed a lot and cut him off completely, I had to make myself move on because if not, I would've kept going back. I changed my number and also cut everyone off that associated with him. I also kept myself busy with work and doing things with my son to not think about him or the situation."

7. S. Mandela

Oklahoma City, Oklahoma

Why did the relationship end?

"We dated for almost a year. The relationship ended because I was tired of the arguing, the fighting and the abuse. I went to your seminar and realized this was not the first nor would it be the last relationship like this unless I realized my self-worth. I remember I had so much love around me that day at your workshop. It literally changed my life forever.

I cannot express how many times I said to myself, "I know my self-worth" over and over and over again. I knew the relationship had to end that day. There was no fixing something that was built without love and without myself knowing my self-worth."

How long did it take you to get over them?

"I cannot remember exactly, but it was more like several months. It doesn't take me long to get over someone. Being hurt over and over makes you immune to that."

What steps did you take to get over them?

"It was hard to end it. I was scared. I didn't know what to say. So I ignored him. That didn't go well. So I knew I would have to end it in person. I called him and told him to come over. I unlocked the door and I hid under my covers like a child. (You know like when the covers are going to protect you from monsters when you are scared) When he came in I said, 'I can't do this anymore I just want to be friends' while under my covers still. He tried to crawl in bed with me, but I didn't let him.

I told him I didn't feel good, I needed rest and that I would call him tomorrow. I was not sick but I was surely sick of him. When he left I was sad but, oh so relieved. It was like weights coming off of my body! We texted here and there for a couple of months. He wanted things to work, but I knew better. I was on to a new start. I knew I had to work on learning and realizing the value of my self-worth and work on never ever forgetting that value again. Thank you so much Egypt you saved my life. :)"

Each person took a different route to reach the same end. If you only follow step one that may be enough for you to get over your ex. Some may not need all the steps or to do them in order before healing. It's a matter of being human. We're not all made the same, nor do we all think, hurt or heal the same. The only important part of this chapter you need to pay attention to is…no one gave up on getting over their ex.

NOTES:

___

You are worthy of love...
Smile Again

www.GetOverThem.com

4/Till Death Do Us Part…Or Extreme Exes.

August 8th 2015: Houston, Texas

- A Texas man broke into his ex's home, handcuffed her alongside her husband, their six children, his own son then fatally shot each victim in the head, authorities said.

August 14th 2015: St. Paul, Minnesota

-Authorities rescued a woman who was being held hostage by her ex-boyfriend. She was able to contact them by making a secret call to 911 after she convinced him that she needed to go to the library.

August 24th 2015: Providence, Rhode Island

-Months after their relationship ended, a man used a gun to end his life and the life of his ex-girlfriend, police confirmed.

What do they all have in common? A person not being able to deal with the end of a relationship. It's bigger than relationships and love. This is about saving lives, healing souls and repairing the damage of horrible teaching in regards to getting over an ex.

Leaders, politicians, doctors, lawyers, teachers,

mothers, fathers and anyone with a beating heart can find themselves dealing with a difficult break up. We all fall in love, get hurt and recycle terrible techniques of recovery.

Who teaches us healthy methods to overcome the pain of cancelled relationships? It's definitely not taught in schools. TV does a poorer job of it by simply romanticizing the journey as a one-week phenomenon of anguish then poof; you're smiling like the person didn't exist.

Movies only show us, "The best way to get over someone is to get under a new person." They're basically donating the thought process, "Sex with a new person will fix your pain." As a result, you inadvertently dismiss the pain you'll bring into a new relationship. Not to neglect all of the scars your new person will have to deal with because of it. This is all a lie.

People are dying, being held captive, murdering and committing suicide all because of one common denominator: an inability to let someone go. No one desires to be part of those stories. What you're doing by reading this book is called, "prevention." Believe it or not, you may have saved yourself from becoming any of the criminals or victims mentioned.

NOTES:

_____
_____
_____
_____
_____
_____
_____
_____
_____
_____
_____
_____
_____
_____
_____
_____

Sadness is temporary...
Smile Again

www.GetOverThem.com

3/When Will You Get Out Of Your Own Way?
Our worst enemy is our attention.

"Just one more mile" is what my mind tells me. "Wait…it's ONE more mile?" is what my legs tell me. There I am, losing my breath en route to being defeated by this hill. As I fight to continue, the hill gets the best of me. Slowing down, something catches my eye. No, this wasn't a beautiful woman or exotic car. It was a dead possum.

Closing in on this site, I began to stare longer than I should. I'm now stuck staring at this lifeless animal. At this moment, I'm well aware how I appear. Each passerby either thinks: **a.)** I want to poke it with a stick or **b.)** I have never seen road kill. Although comical, neither were accurate assessments. I just kept looking.

Honestly, I had no knowledge as to why I was locked into this staring game with an opponent who died before the match started. God's, "Aha!" moment didn't arrive until a few seconds (that felt like minutes) passed.

"Have you ever wondered why a possum rarely makes it over to the sidewalk?" This question beamed into my head yet the answer didn't. The follow up, "Why does it almost always get close to the edge, then gets hit by the car?" Another question, but no answer. Lastly, "The distance between the trees and sidewalk is 15 feet wide. Don't you think a possum can run that in less than a second or two?" I knew the answer to this one. "Of course!" I said aloud. At this moment I'm pretty sure the people looking at me went with: **c)** He's a lunatic talking to a dead possum. Then, I asked myself a couple questions.

"If the possum can run so fast over such short a distance, why did it get to the edge and die? Why didn't it just keep running to the other side? The answer came almost as fast as the questions: the car headlights.

Have you noticed most road kill are nocturnal animals? If they're out during the night, it's mainly because it's safer and their feeding is easier. While this time is best for them to avoid us humans, many don't completely avoid us.

While foraging for the best morsels or attempting to mate, they venture off across the non-busy street and back without much worry. However, when they're scurrying to come back after a night of feeding or mating, they are faced with meeting what they attempted to avoid…us.

As they get closer to the safety of the sidewalk, they see headlights. Instead of making it across, they stare at those lights. Can you imagine they were just a split second away from getting to their *finish line*? Another day of mating and feeding could have been promised if not for a split second of lost focus. Now, they're dead. Is this your story?

Many times we're faced with the simple question with a not so simple answer of: "When will you get out of your own way?" Oddly, most will almost always blame their inability to move on from an ex on the very ex they're attempting to move away from. It's even more unique when instead of using the ammunition of what their ex has done to them as a reason to leave or cease contact; it's used to create an inquiry into the ex's life. This is when we reminisce.

Some find any reason to look at old pictures shared, call the ex's family, visit areas the ex normally is or keep in touch with joint friends they met during the relationship.

At this moment, it is not them keeping you on the hook; it's you hooking yourself.

You have consciously or unconsciously constructed a system of doubt, pain and confusion aimed to keep you from getting over them. The mere idea of it being you keeping you from getting over them is a far-fetched idea to some. Unless the ex is deliberately contacting or creating scenarios to physically see you, who else is at fault?

Before attempting to get over an ex, get over your desire to keep your happiness in the hands of someone who already abandoned it. Before attempting to get over an ex, get over hurting your heart with tours of their images or meetings with friends you've shared. Before attempting to get over an ex…get over yourself. Your heart deserves it.

NOTES:

You deserve happiness...
Smile Again

www.GetOverThem.com

2/Were They Worth Your Tears?
Hint: No…they are not!

What did they do to deserve your tears, hurt or possibly depressive symptoms? An amazing author and friend, Vikki Johnson of **BET Networks** once asked me the above. I had no answer.

At the time I was faced with living without a woman I planned to date. This young lady wasn't even my girlfriend. We never went past the "going on dates" phase. Yet still, she was one of few women my sister approved of.

Just to keep count, my wife is only the third woman in that category. Here's even more of a point: only one of the remaining two was actually a girlfriend. The other woman to be approved by my sister wasn't even a girlfriend for more than two months. Not two years, but months. Yet this one who I cried over was a woman I wanted to be serious with but waited too long.

She was beautiful and Haitian. I've always had a thing for Caribbean women due to their family values. At the time, she went to medical school and was very much into me. To me, she was everything a man could want in a woman. But was she worth my tears, hurt and depression? No, she was not.

No one is. No one deserves to infect you with pain. No matter what side of the coin you land on as it pertains to the victim or violator, the answer is, "No one." Why? Why would they?

Sometimes we date people who don't deserve us. We give them everything but receive little to nothing in return. We aim to love them more than they love themselves but no matter how we try to love or teach them how to love, we fail to receive even a small portion of consistent happiness from our effort.

When that relationship ends, agony owns our hearts. Coupled with the feeling of stupidity for even allowing them in, the depression of such poor judgment seeps into your mind. It's at this time you should ask yourself, "Why am I allowing someone who gave me so little to impact my health so much?"

If the person was the best mate you've ever had, you will mourn their departure because, as stated previously, when you love someone, leaving them is comparable to losing a loved one. When someone dies, we cry because we loved and wish to continue loving them. It would seem inhumane to break up with a genuine friend and go on without a tear or moment or mourning. This isn't to make you less human but to add logic to your journey.

We seldom ask ourselves, "Why am I crying?" or "What did they do to deserve this pain?" If you did, you'll force yourself to answer. Why are you crying? They left, you want them back or can't believe you even allowed them to hurt you? Whatever the answer is, keep asking "Why" after each answer. You will eventually end up with, "No, they are not worth it."

My mother died when I was 12. Prior to her funeral, I honestly believed and prepared to jump in the casket with her. Why? My mourning was powerful. Life without my mother was unlivable. There could be no tomorrow without her. It's impossible to believe there could be. How? She was everything to me: my mother, father, grandmother and grandfather all in one. How could I continue breathing? Was she worth me dying with her? No, she wasn't. There is another story to be told and I have to live to tell it. So do you.

Questioning your tears/grieving is a way to keep everything in perspective. Of course you may cry or hurt but that's natural. What is not as natural or common is being honest with yourself as to why you're hurting or what makes this person deserve such mourning.

The hope behind this is that you will start to unearth answers that give you reasons to heal so that your story can go on. There is another lover not too far away who can love you better than you were loved before. I'm proof of it.

My wife is a gift I've never imagined to have. Even during this writing I'm dumbfounded as to how I managed to meet her. What if I was still in the hurt phase? Crying daily over a woman who I thought loved me wouldn't allow for the next person to come into my life. Who wants to love someone so broken? Not only that, how could I continue to inspire those around me if I never asked, "Does she deserve all this time and tears?"

You are writing a love story on your heart. In most great stories, there are many characters. From Harry Potter to the Holy Bible, everyone has a purpose;

otherwise they wouldn't even have been immortalized in ink. In both of those books, how many characters are spoken of from chapter one until the end? I know for the Holy Bible, it's just one, God.

The love story you're writing will have you as the only recurring character. No matter the amount of people who pop up in this tale, only one may end it with you. As long as you give the power of your pain to one person, you may never see how that story ends. Own the pain and believe that no one deserves to make you feel so ill. Use this as an ability to fight your hurt.

Keep writing that book. It will be hard but never lose yourself in your tears. Why? Someone else needs you to write them in your love story.

NOTES:

Be honest with yourself…
Smile Again

www.GetOverThem.com

1/ Do You Know You?
If you do, you may scare those who don't.

"You won't be anything without me." He yelled as I walked out of the audition room. Not the six words you want to hear from a casting director. The only six words I wanted to hear would be, "Mr. Robinson, you got the part!" I didn't get the latter but my heart wasn't shaken. Why?

There was this woman traveling to Nashville, Tennessee. She wanted to pursue her dreams as a country music star. The only caveat was: she was short, had a thick accent and was Asian. Nothing of her screamed, "You will make it." Despite not fitting the image of a country music star, she dreamed and chased such a dream.

Knowing very little of America, outside of what played on her country music stations, she ventured to hitch hike her way from New York to Nashville. Her plan was to fly to New York and experience the journey of what some of her favorite musicians spoke about on their records. With her thumb up and guitar secure in its box, she prayed that God would assist in helping her avoid any evil drivers. Eventually, she gets picked up.

"Where you going honey?" asked the driver of a Ford F150 pick up. *"I'm going to Nashville. I'm going to be a country music star."* She said. He laughed. They didn't talk much throughout the ride. He was coming from Maine, passing through New York to Pennsylvania. Once in Pennsylvania, he dropped her off at a hotel. The driver didn't ask for a dime just said, with a smirk, "I wish you luck on your dream." The next day, she was outside with her thumb up and guitar secured in its box. Again, she prayed no dangerous driver would pick her up. She gets picked up again.

"So, what you got in that box, a guitar?" The red headed lady in the eighteen-wheeler asked. She responded, *"Yes. I'm going to become a country music star."* The red head didn't laugh, she instead asked, "How?" The young lady replied, *"I'm going to learn better English, learn to sing better, and write the best songs in the world."* The red head smiled and replied, "Well, you look different. That might work to your benefit. Hope you remember us little folk when you become famous." The young lady countered with, *"Of course."*

As they arrived to their destination, the red head didn't ask for a penny, just gave the young lady advice on how to avoid some of the deadbeat American men. Now in North Carolina, she was back in another hotel.

Much like every day prior, she's back outside by the highway with her thumb up and guitar secured in its box. Excited about being one stop away from Nashville, she forgets to pray. A van approaches and she gets picked up.

Inside is a very surly man and his even more unpleasant wife. The first questions asked by his wife are, "Where are you going and how much you got to get there?" The young lady reply, *"I'm going to Nashville. How much will that cost?"* The wife responds with, "$300 cash. We don't trust you hitch hikers with checks." The young lady agrees. The husband asks, "Why Nashville? I didn't know they had many Asian people in Nashville." The young lady says, *"I'm going to become a country music star."* The couple erupts in laughter and banter.

"You can't be that. You're short, you're not that cute and you're Asian. Listen to your accent. You won't make it. I wouldn't buy that mess. Try something else. Maybe dancing or something. This must be some kind of joke. " For the next 7+ hours they belittle her. Making fun of her in the most despicable ways. She reaches Nashville.

Before getting out, the husband says, "Have you ever heard of the little engine that could?" The young lady replied, *"Yes, I heard of -"* He cuts her off and says, "Well you can't and you ain't no engine!" With a face unshaken by his words, she asked, *"Have you ever heard of the GPS story?"*

Caught off guard, the husband says, "No." She begins the story:

"There was this African warrior sentry in charge of alerting the Addae kingdom of when an enemy approached. One day he saw the Sankofa, their neighboring enemies, preparing to invade. He could see their camp roughly a mile away. After disclosing the incident to his tribe, he then tells them, 'Trust me, we must go to the Sankofa kingdom and give up this one.' He was so sure and confident that most followed his seemingly insane advice. However, some mocked him and decided to stay so they can defend the Addae kingdom.

Taking an alternate route, which evaded the Sankofa warriors from noticing them, the Addae tribe reached their enemy's kingdom. They found it guarded by captives from different tribes who also lost their kingdoms to the Sankofa. They too didn't like the enemy. The warrior convinced all captives to fight with his tribe. Together, they far outnumbered the Sankofa.

The new regime of Addae and former slaves constructed creative ways to ambush the Sankofa's. In short time, they made the surrounding area a death zone with secret pit falls at every turn. Expert bowmen readied their weapons to kill the Sankofa before they reached within striking distance. The Addae were ready for battle.

Unsuspecting the danger in their future, the Sankofa were now heading back to their kingdom.

After a swift victory over only a few Addae fighters back at the Addae kingdom, the Sankofa were joyful as they journeyed to their own kingdom. On their way, many booby traps cut them down before they even reached the gates. When they finally made it to their kingdom gates, awaiting them were angry yet well-prepared captives and warriors from the Addae kingdom.

The battle was short and the Addae were victorious. Not only did the Sankofa lose their kingdom and the Addae kingdom, now they were captives to those they once enslaved. When the people asked the warrior, "How did you know to come here and why were you so confident despite those people mocking you?" He responded, ***"I trust my fighting skills and followed my G.P.S, God's Positional System. He directed my steps and victory only occurs when you follow God. My confidence comes from my faith and knowing I'm talented at battle. I know me and trust what I believe in. No amount of negativity would change how I feel about my destination or me."***

The husband and wife laughed then the wife said, "Well, whatever GPS you got should be amazing. Shoot, I may follow it one day too. Please give me my money and follow your God, honey."

After handing them the money, she smiles and says, *"Thank you for helping me begin the journey of chasing my dream."* The couple is caught off guard by her genuine joy and kindness. Rather than the customary, "You're welcome," they utter, "You better get yourself a map of better dreams so you can chase a different one. Nothing about you will be successful here." They speed off laughing. She smirks and reaches the office of Lemore Records. A new label created by her cousin solely to fill the high demand of country music for the Asian community.

The map of her dreams was right. Yet, despite running into negative people, she journeyed on. How so? She knew herself. She took time to learn about her goals, hobbies and why she did certain things. This made her faith more secure because she knew what she could handle. Do you?

Most people don't know themselves. They don't know why their favorite food is their favorite food outside of, "It tastes good." Many can't detail why they keep dating the same type of people. Even more wild, most will not date and use the, "I have to get to know myself" as a reason to avoid dating….but never "get to know themselves." Why?

We don't know and aren't taught how to get to know ourselves. We live in a world of instant gratification. It's now now now. Nothing is left for tomorrow and everything is more appealing today. Did you know that every sale repeats itself? Almost every, "If you miss out today, you will never see it again" happens at least twice a year. Your sanity needs time and isn't a discount or bargain that can be rushed.

When it comes to getting to know yourself, it's about asking questions you may feel uncomfortable asking. Here are a few to start your journey as it relates to getting over an ex:

1. What can you do to make YOU happy?

2. What hobbies did you miss during the relationship?
3. What makes you a great boyfriend/girlfriend? Name 20 things.
4. Do you fear never being loved again, if so why?
5. Do you love you, if so can you name 20 things you love about you?

This is just a few but honestly taking time away from everyone and talking to yourself is a powerful way of getting to know you. It's not just about answering a few questions but finding time to spend with you and understanding how to make you happy.

When you're able to make yourself happy, it changes how you incorporate others into your life. You find it weird to add unhealthy thinkers into your inner circle. Those who won't add to your happiness become more parasitic than anything. Finally, you find out one of the best loves you'll ever experience: self- love.

Here is an actual route to asking yourself those previous questions and ways to get to know yourself.

- **Step 1.** Etch out a moment for just spending time on you. This doesn't have to be a day or weekend. It can even take 10-15 minutes. Here's the catch: you can't use the computer or any device that may take you away from focusing on you.

- **Step 2.** Pick something to think about. Example: What's your favorite ice cream and why? Where would you like to travel and why? These may seem like little questions but the "Why" drives home its importance to you.

- **Step 3.** Write your answers down in a journal. Use actual paper and pencil. This helps with getting you away from potentially distracting technology.

- **Step 4.** Do this routinely. You set the schedule. Maybe this is weekly or daily. Maybe you want this to be an outing so it's monthly. No matter the fact, you set it as something you normally do. Why? You will do this your entire life. We all change and we all get better. I used to love steak, now my favorite food is chicken wings. Why? I changed as I aged.

You'll find that this is one of the most amazing experiences you can ever imagine. Most people don't know themselves and rely on others to decipher why they do certain things. Hence why some people can't actually answer the age-old question of, "Why did you do that?" It's almost always answered with, "I don't know." You know why they don't know? They don't know who they are and/or never asked themselves such a question.

When the casting director told me, "You won't be anything without me." I honestly laughed on the inside. No, I wasn't cocky. There wasn't anything about my talent to make me believe, "You'll see me in the future because I'm the next super star!" That wasn't needed. My only needs are knowing how hard I work, who I pray to and what I'm made of. In short, since I knew me, their words didn't dictate my present or future emotional state.

Talk to yourself. Learn why you love you or why you don't. Write a book about what you love about you. Even if one day you don't give this book to your husband or wife, at least you will always know who you are.

NOTES:

Be bold on your journey to joy...
Smile Again

www.GetOverThem.com

Ten Steps To Get Over Your Ex...FOR GOOD!
Countdown over...You're ready.

Step #1: Stop ALL COMMUNICATION!
No email, calls, social networking sites (Delete their connection) and texts.

Why You Should:

This is VERY important. You can't get over someone you still talk to. Further conversation will only put you further in pain or confusion. Why? Sometimes we get lulled into believing, "There's a future" or "Maybe I was wrong about them", etc. This only occurs because now you've allowed the healing to cease and the wound to expand.

Have you ever been cut and while bleeding, spread the cut open? Odds are no but if you did, it would hurt more than it originally did. As a matter of fact, you might feel extraordinary pain. Why? The pain was new and at its peak. You took it to another level. Therefore, you will feel the extra pain but it's *self-inflicted*.

What happens next is as you begin to heal, you'll notice the scar is much larger than before. The injury will take longer to heal and you'll know this to be true…by the tattoo left on your heart.

If you are "Getting over them", talking to them is regression. Especially if it's an intimate or innuendo laced conversation where you know it's much more than just, "talk." If you can't do this, get ready for hurt. This is a lesson I learned from my older sister, Chasity Walker.

Now, if you're parenting a child, roommates or work together, that doesn't mean, "He's not talking about me or my situation." No, you can still communicate cordially and leave out personal information. Here are some examples:

Roommates:

You can discuss the bills, house party/house warming plans…etc. Leave out who's dating who and one another's social activities. If this is hard, start your journey to leave the location. There's no need to live with someone if you can't handle them moving on.

Parenting a child:

You can discuss what you two will do with the child and everything relating to the child. When you start to dig into their relationship life, you're digging to go back, not forward. If they're dating, that's their life. It's not easy, it won't be but it's life. If you don't master this, you won't be able to move on.

<u>Co-Workers:</u>

You can discuss work related subjects but leave the personal at home or after work hours. The more you play, " I can handle talking about their new relationship or life without me" the more you're double-dutching over hot coals.

Why This Is Hard:

"They have a birthday coming up." "Their mother is in the hospital", "I don't want to be rude and ignore them." or the INFAMOUS "I'm mature enough to be friends." All of this is toxic thinking. You two were together. You two were in love. You two were special. Now it's over. A habit is broken and you'll fight tooth and nail to find a way to recommit to some form of it.

When you said, "I love you" that was supposed to be a forever statement. This is why it's hard to do step one. You love them. They loved you. It wasn't supposed to end. Now that's it's over, ending communication so you can heal seems like an "evil" idea. It isn't.

You don't need to have updates about their life because you know what... they are having fun. Most people aren't moping around and posting sad images or statuses via social media. That's not going to happen. Why? Most people have dignity and/or pride. Allowing the world to see their pain isn't ideal. Therefore when you check their updates and see them at a mall, party, or pool, you'll be devastated.

Simultaneously, not seeing those images will leave you barren because…you just want to know. Well, you don't need to know and honestly knowing will hurt you more than not knowing.

You will make any and every excuse not to do step one. No excuse will be logical since they all come from your heart and not your mind. Why speak to someone who is no longer your mate? Friends take time apart to heal during bad arguments. Take time apart or suffer a broken heart that never heals.

Bad Advice Many Follow:
"I need to keep in contact just in case _____"

Oddly, the bad advice most follow will come from themselves. Example: *"No, I have to keep in contact with their mother. Their mother is like a mother to me."* No…they are not like a mother to you. They didn't birth you. They didn't breastfeed or nurse you. They loved or liked you while you dated their real child. However, this isn't to negate any real relationships built.

We also follow the false truth of, "I'm not a mean person. I just can't cut someone off." Yes you can. Yes you should. What is mean in saying, "I need to get away from you so I can heal and be loved by someone new?" There is nothing mean in that. However, if the ex makes you feel as though that's mean, you will only realize how mean they're being.

Lastly, the bad advice can come from the ex. "I thought we are friends. How can you just leave a friend?" No, you two *were* friends. Past tense. Once you're out of a relationship with someone who was more courting you than befriending you, how can you still carry on a friendship?

It wasn't a friendship. That was a courtship. A courtship is when a man chases a woman to show he's worthy of her hand in marriage. However, once that's over...that's it.

Now, in some cases there was actually a true, platonic friendship built. You two knew and grew up together, then fell in love. That has more of a steady foundation of a friendship worth saving. However, once you're over, remember you still have to heal. The same person giving you the heartbreak can't also be your heart surgeon. Stepping away from a friend should be met with mutual support not guilt.

When you're healed, in a new relationship and no longer wanting a relationship with the ex, communication should come slow and with purpose. Until then, avoid any connection because when hurt, you are your heart's worst enemy.

NOTES:

Do not give up...
Smile Again

www.GetOverThem.com

Step #2: INDUCE Thinking About Them.

Yes, keep them on your mind!

Why You Should:

Consistently have conversations about the relationship (with friends or family) and what went right in addition to wrong. Remember the good times and reminisce on the bad. Talk about them with friends. Sooner or later…something amazing will occur.

You will alienate your friends and they will display subtle signs of their dismay. Eventually you will get SICK of the THOUGHT of your ex.

Believe it or not, you will get tired of talking about them. Thinking about them will grow boring and bothersome. No one will want to hear another thing about your ex. Neither will you. This gives your brain a break from the breakup.

When an ex leaves or you leave an ex, what they do, who they're doing it with and how they're doing it is a constant update your mind desires. Thoughts of "Do they have a new partner?", "Are they just as sad as I am?" and "Are they out partying or sulking?" can cloud your to do list…quick. Indulge those thoughts. You will get tired of them. Trust me.

Think about your favorite movie. Can you honestly watch it every day? You may think you can, but if you watch Avatar (A movie I LOVE, by the way) 10 times a day, it will lose its affect. You will stop watching and when it's on TV, you'll bypass it. (I do so now)

You need to get to a place where thinking about them doesn't affect your day, mood or agenda. Simply ignoring their existence in your mind is far too difficult when you two shared so many moments together. There are a multitude of places you visited, favorite meals shared and movies watched. Embrace those instances; let the tears or anger flow. Before you know it…you won't care about what movie you watched together…it would just be a movie.

Why This Is Hard:

You're doing it now. Therefore, it's hard to believe this is an effective solution to your problem. I'm not asking you to simply think about them. I'm asking you to purposely think about them for the sole reason of being sickened by the thought of them. Rather than random moments of reminiscing, I want you to control those thoughts.

Your mind is being stimulated to think about them based on instances of hearing or viewing items, locations or people you two commonly know. You aren't planning these moments of nostalgia. It's a reaction. You have no power over that.

Think about them now. Right now. How much time you shared. How much pain the break up caused. How your family felt when it was over. How your friends had to comfort you. While you hold those thoughts…make the choice to say, "It's over."

It's hard to do this. You may still want them or they may still want you. If you don't induce your thoughts of them, then the sporadic moments of times shared may haunt you. Either own the choice of remembering or become a slave to memories.

Bad Advice Many Follow:

"I can't keep thinking about them, otherwise it will drive me crazy." (Ironically, this is typically done while you are actually thinking about them.)

As like most bad advice, it typically comes from oneself. Instead of thinking about them with the purpose of being burdened by thinking of them, we still do it to find a way back. Here are the classic thoughts: "Maybe the reason we broke up wasn't that serious", "You know what, I should give them another chance", "Why would I allow something so small ruin all of the memories?" "They may never do it again."

Any and all of the above are excuses to inflict more undeserved damage to your mind, heart and spirit. Thinking about them shouldn't be a method of torture to remember the horrible things they've done; nor should it be an expedition in search of ways they've made you smile. You should do this to realize maybe the journey was meant to be over because you've experienced enough with this person.

The best advice you can give yourself is to not trust your instincts. You are designed to be flawed and make mistakes. It says so in the Holy Bible.

Ecclesiastes 7:20

Indeed, there is no one on earth who is righteous, no one who does what is right and never sins.

In the end, you are the sum of your experiences. Some experiences don't need to be re-experienced. Think about them and get filled with the urge to forget reliving those moments. Become numb to the thought of a future with them…then smile.

NOTES:

Expect to find peace...
Smile Again

www.GetOverThem.com

Step #3: Ban SEX/Intimacy WITH THEM!
If sex/intimacy could keep them…it would've kept them.

Why You Should:

Some people think: "If you give it to them, they will miss it and come back" **This is sad and false!**

If you're having sex with them for revenge…it won't work. If you're having sex with them for mutual pleasure…it won't work. If you're having sex with them to get them back…it won't work.

Revenge sex is comparable to threatening your landlord with the words, "I'll pay you more and live somewhere else!" It's not effective. Sex is pleasure. Why give them pleasure as a form of revenge? No, you're not aiming to get revenge; you're really seeking an avenue back into their lives. If not, it's still a horrible idea.

Mutual pleasure is a lie. Yes, their sex could've been AMAZING but…how dare you subject yourself to being an option to a person who once held you as a priority? Where is the integrity in such thinking? You now hold no expectation of loyalty from them. Even if they say they're not having sex with anyone…why believe them? They have no reason to be honest. You're just an ex now.

Think about it. You could be one of many people they're sleeping with.

Why open yourself to potential STD's or even a child? Do you think having a child with someone you're not married to or dating is wise? Many children are now part of a single parent household because of this thought, "A baby will keep them." No, it doesn't. A baby keeps them in your life but never in the place you want them to be. Don't believe me? Ask a single parent who is either sick of the other parent's presence or jealous of their absence.

Sex to get them back is pointless. It's another terrible move to get someone who left or you left back into a relationship. You mean to tell me you think they'll come back for something they already had? Let's make it plain.

If you left McDonald's…could they get you back by offering you a Big Mac? The same Big Mac you ate everyday before you quit or were fired? No, it's just a poor excuse to put your heart in danger of being broken beyond repair. Let's get deeper.

Imagine this, you two enjoy a passionate moment of sweet, slow or rough sex. The next day you decide to call to say "hi", but they don't pick up the phone. You text, "Good morning"…no reply. You leave a voicemail and they don't call you back. You're upset! You call more, text more and wait more…still no response. Fed up, you check their social media…they're out with their "friend" having a ball.

After seeing this, you're in a rage! Just hours ago you gave your body to them. How DARE they spend time with someone else? A new person? What about you? Well…what about you? Who are you? You're just an ex they're having sex with. Nothing more.

Why put yourself in that position? You don't have to.

Why This Is Hard:

It's hard to believe something so sacred wouldn't be powerful enough to bring them back. Even the innocent, "It's just sex" is a bad route to take.

If they already had it before and left you after getting it, why would it entice them to come back? Your "donation" won't inspire them to date you again. At the very LEAST you will become a well-respected "booty call." Think about it.

It's hard to believe your body isn't special enough to retain someone. It isn't. If it was, why did they leave? Sex isn't as important as we make it to be. Why? We make it too important. We place too much emphasis on it. So much so that it becomes a means to an end instead of a part of a journey.

In my life, I've never seen a person come back because of sex. Once, a friend of mine told me she enticed an ex to visit her so she could have sex with him. She went into detail on how she did everything he would enjoy; pushing him to reach levels of pleasure he's never received. After they climaxed…she left.

The purpose? To make him miss her. The result? They never dated again...nor did he mention anything about missing her. The true ending? Her ex received a free sexual experience...from someone he didn't want anymore.

> If you're just looking for sex, ask yourself this, "Is 5-10 minutes of pleasure worth my dignity?"

Bad Advice Many Follow:
"Maybe one more time will remind them of what they're missing and they'll want to come back."

"Hey, it's just one more time. What's the harm?" Normally this advice comes from friends, the ex or yourself. This idea that one more time is, "harmless" is pretty ironic since most regrets only take one time to become a regret.

The aforementioned friend of mine bragged about, "Giving it to him" as revenge. This is a real life experience of using the poor, "One more time" mantra to get them back. She was so descriptive and determined that one would believe it could really work.

Her plan was to give him everything he always wanted sexually and maybe some things she didn't do with him. He was in for a treat. What she described to me…would make the most happily single man want to consider changing his status. This woman had her plan figured out. How did it end? It failed.

She's not with him. He now enjoyed a beautiful moment of bliss without commitment and…what? How did she feel? How was her heart after this engagement? Was she always a woman who could do one-night stands? No.

She is a queen: a very beautiful, highly educated and faithful woman. But she listened to her own awful advice, which resulted in more pain. Don't listen to you. Listen to logic. Sex won't make you feel better. At least not the "better" you truly crave.

NOTES:

You deserve happiness...
Smile Again

www.GetOverThem.com

Step #4: Remember…You Are An EX!
Act accordingly.

Why You Should:
Imagine this...

One day, your mother asks you to sit down with her. In her hands is an aged and torn burgundy bound book. She opens it. Inside, you see beautiful pictures of you and her as youth. In the photo, she's 20 and you're 2. Your smile widens but then you notice that you two aren't the only people in the photos.

As you continue to flip through the photos, there is an older lady who keeps popping up. In many cases, she's the prominent figure in the image. The last page shows all three of you laughing. The lady is sitting next to your mother and your mother is holding you.

Your mother then says to you, *"Do you know that lady?"* You reply, "No, I don't." Your mother replies, *"That's our mother. I'm your sister. She died when we were younger. I've been taking care of you to honor a promise I made to her. Now, I'm your sister so call me "Sis". You're now old enough to handle yourself so you no longer have to rely on me."*

Even if you have an other worldly imagination, you're still probably thinking, "This couldn't happen to me." You're right. This is a rare incidence. However, you can no longer call your sister, "momma" because now you know your role and she knows hers. An odd story but the point remains.

How does this relate to step 4? Once you know your position…you have to stay in it. Otherwise, you're lying to yourself and wasting the other person's valuable time in being honest with you about your position.

You're not allowed to visit the family unannounced. You're not allowed to pop up to their house for late night visits. You're not allowed to borrow their car. You're not allowed to assume Holidays will be spent with them. You're just not allowed anymore. Therefore, you shouldn't. If you do, all embarrassment endured will be your fault, not theirs.

Remind yourself, "It is over" and don't allow yourself to still engage in "relationship" benefits. You can't worry about who they are dating, having sex with or calling. Don't check their phones or go through their stuff. Understand your position and accept it. If not, be ready for hurt when reminded of who you are to them.

Why This Is Hard:

Going from all to nothing is a difficult transition. You had access to so much to now experience restriction is unnatural. In your mind, you may believe you should have liberty to still enjoy certain things such as birthdays, family gatherings and the like. Honestly, you don't and shouldn't. You are no longer theirs. You're just an ex. In some cases, you are not a friend anymore.

Don't use, "I'm a friend" as a reason to gain some privilege. Abusing a friendship with an ex is a sure fire way to get you blocked from their life…for good.

This is supposed to be hard. You weren't meant to experience this side (single) again. A breakup is always unexpected until it happens. Now you have to adjust. Smile, it will get better.

Bad Advice Many Follow:

"If we're 'friends with benefits', I get the same access as I used to. Maybe this will mature into a full relationship again.

"Well, once mine always mine." "Friends should still get access to each others daily routine." "Just because it's over doesn't mean everything has to end." This should be the soundtrack of most horror films right before the villain comes and chases the young campers. This idea is scary and only leads to more confusion. Why?

They are no longer yours. They were never yours. We live in a very possessive time when people have not been taught that you cannot own a person. They were your mate, not your slave. Once they're gone, they're gone.

Friends have access to what their friends allow them to gain access to. None of my friends know the daily routine I undergo. They're my friends but they don't always know who I'm dating and where I'm taking them. They're friends, not employees I give status updates.

Although this part is difficult, understand that it's mandatory. You owe it to your sanity not to live in the past. Think about how great the next relationship will be or how your upcoming vacation on that beach will soothe your urge to swim. Think about something other than lying to yourself.

This is necessary.

NOTES:

_____

_____

_____

_____

_____

_____

_____

_____

_____

_____

_____

_____

_____

_____

_____

Keep reading. Your future self will thank you…
Smile Again

www.GetOverThem.com

Step #5: Remind Yourself WHY It Ended…Then Accept It.

There was a reason…remember it.

Why You Should:

Many people deceive themselves about this. When it is over, take an opportunity to confidently and realistically comprehend why it did not work. Take REAL time. Sit alone, sip tea and contemplate why this person or even you yourself stopped the movement of passion. This is truly important.

If you don't take this time, you will run the risk of committing the same mistake of not paying attention to the telltale signs, leading right back to hurt again. My story is proof.

One woman started acting outside of character, and then she ended up cheating. I knew something was wrong but I didn't act fast enough. The next woman did the same and ended up cheating too. I didn't act fast enough on both accounts. However, I had to sit back and analyze what scenarios are repetitive to avoid them in new relationships.

I not only revisited what occurred in the relationship but the type of person I was in general and also within the relationship. Who was I? What's my "type"? Was she really someone I could build a future with or was she a "work in progress"? I had to think about that. You have to do the same.

Figure out what went wrong, why it went wrong and was the wrong a "right thing". Sometimes when a toxic relationship ends, no matter how it ends, it was a "right thing." Some people are meant to enter and exit, while others are meant to be in your life forever. That choice is yours to make.

Doing this will also keep you honest about the potential of there being a future with the ex. If they cheated, lied or betrayed you, you should ask yourself "If this is what they did when they loved or cared deeply for me, what would they do if I bring them back?" Think about it.

Why This Is Hard:

We like…no…we LOVE to hope for the best in bad people or situations. In many cases, even the harshest circumstance or person will find benefit from our desire for a positive outlook. What do I mean?

Example: If they're consistently verbally abusive. One day, you decide to walkaway because of the abuse. Without hesitation, the abuser will say something to the extent of, "My father verbally abused me, that's why I abuse you." If not that, it will be some form of a phenomenal origin story for their actions. Odds are, you will now reject what was done and settle with "making it work." Why? We want to make it work even though we know it's not or never has been what we wanted. This is also what happens when we don't lean on what made us an ex to begin with.

Using the previous example, you have to remember why they hurt you. That's what an adult did to another adult. This wasn't an accident. You're not on earth to be a physical, verbal or spiritual punching bag. Why endure the pain again? Why give them another chance? Why?

We are programmed, in many cases, to look for the best in a person. Even if that person has displayed the worst imaginable actions, we're still optimistic.

Remember, people don't break up because everything was perfect and perfection was insatiable. People breakup because something went wrong and fixing it was too difficult to accomplish.

Additionally, the idea of an "end" to something that was supposed to be "forever" is a hard pill to swallow. Reminding ourselves of why it ended is actually soothing. It creates a sense of completion to the thought. The truly arduous part is leaving it at "Why is it over?" and not "How can I fix the problem to get them back?" Don't fix it. Just remind yourself that if it were fixable, it wouldn't have ended.

Bad Advice Many Follow:
"Every ending is a new beginning. We can forget the past and work on the present."

Ever hear of the "hopeless romantic"? That's not solely for the person who just loves to love. It's also for the person who really hopes for romance even in the face of dead-end love. Don't allow your hopelessness to be a flaw.

If your best didn't keep them, I can honestly predict your "better than best" won't. Why? You two ended it for a reason. Even if it was emotionally charged or logical, it was a decision to terminate this union. Why didn't you or they give your/their best when things were good?

If the answer is, "I have to do better" why weren't you motivated to do better when you had an oyster in your hand? What made you wait until the pearl was no longer there for you to recognize the need to cherish this gift with your all? These are questions your ex mate is probably asking you, and probably what you should ask yourself.

There isn't a good enough reason for the "try harder" advice. Why? During a relationship, your mate will or has told you how your actions made them feel. Maybe they're at fault and you told them how their repetitive actions made you feel. This is an almost universal action for mostly sane people.

People who have integrity and know their worth are unapologetic about checking someone who mistreats them. It's not uncommon for a person to say, "I don't like it when you do ____." Some brush it off or try to fix it but no matter the case, the attempt can't be taken for granted.

They gave you or you gave them an opportunity to do better than your/their best. The, "I'll try" didn't work or maybe it was never really met with genuine priority. Therefore, trust was lost. Not betrayal but the trust in your/their word. If a coach let you shoot nine times in a game and you missed all nine, why would they let you shoot a 10th? Why, because you'll try harder?

Why didn't you try harder the first nine times? What's the difference now? You have more motivation because the game is on the line? Now under immense pressure you will all of a sudden become a pro at shooting? Why couldn't you do it well when there was no pressure? These aren't jabs but real things to think about.

Trying harder is a boat you or they missed. Don't worry about catching it or them missing it. Just try hard every single day with the next love and/or pray you'll meet someone who will. They'll benefit more from your work ethic. Why? They'll only see a diligent person aiming to love them better than their best everyday…not just lying about trying.

NOTES:

Face your fears…
Smile Again

www.GetOverThem.com

Step #6: Realize You Are Broken.

"Fake It Till You Make It"…doesn't apply here

Why You Should:

Last week I ate some fine Haitian food and *added 3-4 month old Haitian spice called, pikliz* to the rice. Now, I don't know the shelf life of pikliz but I'm sure 3-4 months is way past it. Nevertheless, I devoured this meal. The rice, boulet and pikliz tasted like a gift in my mouth. Now, what happened to my stomach wasn't a gift, blessing or anything positive.

Not even ten minutes passed by and I was married to the toilet. Moments later I vomited one of possibly 30 times. It was a nightmare. How could something so good…go so wrong? It got to a point I was rushed to the emergency room. About five hours later, I was no longer vomiting. The worst was behind me. Literally.

The diarrhea was nagging. My physician instructed me to not eat any fried food and only eat soft non-complicated meals. Chicken noodle soup and Gatorade…that's all I heard. Even with this new regimen, I would still have diarrhea. I just wanted to be my old self. Fed up with this bothersome condition, I said, "I'm just going to eat whatever I want."

Moments later, I'm eating baked chicken, rice, cereal and almost anything I could find. What happened next? I was almost back in the hospital. Why? I wasn't ready. I was still broken. I was still in no condition to treat my stomach how I have in the past. Although this story was a bit yucky, it holds its point.

Many think they are ready to date immediately post breakup but are not. This makes the healing process more painful. Not only are you still hurting but you also run the risk of damaging another who just wants to love you. You have to understand that you are not at 100% yet, so act accordingly.

It's not always about the other person you'll hurt or yourself but the very idea of love you'll destroy just based on your inability to wait. Humans do more harm to themselves than any conspiracy theory could.

We're the same people who will damn a weed smoker while filling a prescription for painkillers, buying a pack of cigarettes or eating any kind of fast food with no hesitation. We like to point fingers at what others are doing while using our other hand to inflict harm on ourselves. Hurting ourselves is a skill we own. Unfortunately we are experts at it.

Being honest with yourself can change the very dynamic of your situation. Why act like you're ready for steak when you can barely handle a bowl of chicken soup? It will only make the recovery process more irksome.

Say it, "I am hurt." This isn't motivational writing. This is purposeful help. Say it to yourself, "I am hurt." Why should you say it? The same reason I should have kept eating chicken noodle soup…to heal and not lie to oneself.

Why It Will Be Hard:

A teacher walks into a classroom. He asks, "Who wants to be broken, raise your hand?" None of the students raise their hands. Why? Simply, no one wants to be broken. Anyone who's endured that journey would want to forget. You have to acknowledge it or something worse may happen.

"I can't love you!" those words haunt me until this day. No, a woman didn't say this to me. No, I didn't say this to a woman, at least not with my voice. I said this with my actions.

While faking it like I was whole, I brutally injured a woman with my moment of brokenness. You see, this scenario wasn't all bad. At least I was honest with my current inability to date her with the proper mindset needed to love her correctly. Honestly, the fault existed in my desire to still date her…period.

What woman would want to date a man as a friend? That's not a relationship, that's just playing a game of, "Like me but don't tell anyone." She deserved more but I sincerely couldn't offer it. This woman was kind, beautiful and brilliant. She met any and every characteristic of a woman I could love. I just wasn't ready to love her. One day, she wrote me a letter.

In that letter, she *probably* disclosed how happy she was with me and how I made her feel special. She *probably* wrote about the wild topics we talked about and how she enjoyed the piggyback rides I gave her. She *probably* detailed many things…but I ripped up the letter so I could never find out. I was honest with her about not being ready to date but not honest with myself about being broken. Faking it hurt someone.

Being broken doesn't prevent people from wanting to love you. It's hard to admit you're too broken to love. Although it's a phase, you will only cause yourself harm by ignoring the importance of this experience. You are not whole, but it's okay. There are others who will come along and love you. It took me three years just to fully come to terms with my damage. This will take time.

A Mercedes with a broken windshield is still a Mercedes. It's just not ready to be driven yet. Why? How dangerous would it be for not only the driver, but also those who are close to the Mercedes? You are still valuable and worthy of the energy God spent on making you. Take this time to cherish your inner and outer beauty. Confess your brokenness and start the healing process.

Bad Advice Many Follow:

"If I act like nothing is wrong, then I'll trick myself into believing nothing is wrong."

When we act as if we're ready to get back on the horse, we secretly say to another person, "I'm going to hurt you. Either you'll stay until I no longer hurt you or I'll hurt you so much, you will eventually hurt someone else." This is what happens when we follow traditionally false advice.

I've mentioned this before, but it's crucially necessary that I mention it again, *"Getting over a new person by getting under an old person"* is a horrible idea. When you use another person to heal your wounds, it's comparable to using a knife to cure a headache. The results won't be desirable.

Yes, it hurts to wallow in despair about your current condition. Yes, it hurts to accept you're broken. Yes, there is nothing fun about any of this step. No, there is nothing powerful about lying to yourself or future mate about your heart's condition. You owe it to yourself to be honest. How else can you have control over your direction?

My consistent goal in this book is to focus on what you can do to fix you. Not a new mate or anyone else. You. You hold the key to making yourself whole. Between you and God, there isn't another person/being who should care more about your well-being. Therein lies the power of change. It's you making a decision to say, "Yes, I'm broken but I'll be whole again because I deserve to be whole again." That's power! You own it.

NOTES:

Happiness is a choice. Choose it...
Smile Again

www.GetOverThem.com

Step #7: Consult Guidance From An Elder or Mentor.
Your hurt isn't unique…

Why You Should:

"I love her and we'll be together forever." Those words, believe it or not, came from middle school age "Egypt." "I love her and we'll be together forever." More words from high school age "Egypt." "I'm going to marry her." Once again, those words came from college age "Egypt" At the time, all of those statements were true to me. To my elders, those words were just laughable.

Why laugh at something I was so sincere about? The reason was that they know a little about the premature proclamation of "forever" and "I love you." They've been on the receiving end of an, "I told you so" and felt its unfavorable sting. Without a doubt, my genuine belief was just comedy to them. How? Since they have been my age and I haven't been theirs, they already saw this movie…maybe too many times.

Elders are full of scars created by bad decisions and moments where they should have listened but refused to. Not only have they made subtle mistakes countless times, they have also found a way to get over it. Following their advice is like having a cheat sheet to life. Think about it; if you didn't study for a test, had no knowledge of the material yet someone gave you all the answers, would you use them? The Holy Bible and Otto Van Bismarck both answer accordingly.

"Only a fool learns from his own mistakes. The wise man learns from the mistakes of others."-Otto Von Bismarck

"The way of fools seems right to them, but the wise listen to advice." Proverbs 12:15

It's not that they're perfect and no longer make similar horrible decisions. Age doesn't bring about perfection. Also, it's not wise to use their current relationship errors or negative behaviors as a way to detail the truth in an obvious spurt of advice. We all will gain new mistakes and blunders as we age. It's the way of the world. The goal isn't to become perfect but become perfect at not making the same mistakes.

How to pick an elder/mentor:

One of the most difficult parts of this journey is selecting someone you respect to donate great advice. I use, "donate" to illustrate how advice should be given. Not as mandatory but as a gift to your life. In regards to respectable advisors, first in mind would be persons of faith, community leaders and teachers. If you're not surrounded by people who you respect, I offer you a different approach.

Rather than someone you respect, look for someone who has endured this issue before and successfully surpassed this phase. Respect their process. This helps you evade trusting them on life advice or any advice outside of just getting over an ex. Many institutions of higher learning have counselors you can visit for free. Even if you don't attend the college/university, you can ask them for referrals of available external counselors to assist your journey of healing. Also, don't count out your parents or relatives.

Parents and family are full of bad decisions, experience and wisdom. You probably know more about their errors than anyone. Remember, even though you may not trust their life decisions, you can trust the advice they give as it relates to getting over an ex.

Ironically, some of the people you gain advice from may not even follow their own advice. That's okay. Sometimes you get the best instruction from someone who wished they followed their own advice. Why? How are your eating habits? Tell me about your workout habits? What about your study habits? How are your saving and investing habits? Are you doing all that you can in terms of your faith walk? Inside all of those questions should be areas where you can do more or better. Even more so, I can guarantee you may advise others on things you wish you would do instead of exactly what you're doing now.

Listen to them and accept their thoughts. I am proof it works. My sister's advice helped me create this book without knowing so. Her words inspired me to grow out of my shame and pain. Now her words are helping you. She's my elder.

Why It Will Be Hard:

If finding an elder is the hardest part, you're lucky. Many times the most difficult part is being willing to expose yourself. Being vulnerable is a challenge. Daring to go in front of the mirror and declare, "It's actually over" is by far the toughest of this journey for many. Asking for help is an act of courage. You're already ahead of the game because many people aren't brave enough to admit they need it.

The advent of social media makes it somewhat easier to disclose our current emotional situation to the world. Easy and wise are two different words. While you may be able to reach the masses with your, "I can't believe it's over" or "Whew, single again" messages, the people who comment aren't always trained in the art of teaching properly. Honestly, the best person to speak with may be the same person who you know will give you an, "I told you so." Maybe it's the person who initially said, "They aren't right for you." No matter who they are, ask and listen.

You don't have to follow all of their advice; it's okay to be selective. Having an elder saves you the trouble of doing what they've done and being even more broken. If you think you can't hurt anymore, just watch what happens when you don't listen to wise counsel. My sister once told me, "Leave her alone." I didn't…then it took another two years to get over her, which took two years out of my life. Just listen.

Bad Advice Many Follow:

"I can do it myself. I don't need anyone. I didn't need anyone to get in the relationship. Won't need anyone to get over it."

I was once told, "There is nothing more foolish than a fool who thinks they're wise." When we find ourselves heartbroken, some become the fool they never imagined becoming. One of the biggest exposing factors is how we communicate our hurt. We honestly believe we can manage this without anyone else.

It's at this time some neglect to pray and others isolate themselves from civilization. Both actions almost always equate to depression. You, in essence, become a fool to your pain. Listening only to yourself and avoiding wise counsel can lead you into a pain you wouldn't wish on an enemy. Don't become the fool the Holy Bible speaks of.

Stay away from a fool, for you will not find knowledge on their lips.
-Proverbs 14:7

Do not answer a fool according to his folly, or you yourself will be just like him.

-Proverbs 26:4

The fear of the LORD is the beginning of knowledge, but fools despise wisdom and instruction.
-Proverbs 1:7

Do not speak to fools, for they will scorn your prudent words.
-Proverbs 23:9

NOTES:

Quitting now will only guarantee failure…
Smile Again

www.GetOverThem.com

Step #8: Have Fun!!

Create or finish that bucket list and remember, "*A smile is free medicine.*"

Why You Should:

When you're sick and act sick, your sickness becomes overwhelmingly difficult to imagine coming to an end. When you at least think of positive things while sick, you feel better. No, you're not faking but rather looking for the good in a bad situation.

"Look on the bright side" are five of the most haunting words to **a.)** Anyone going through a difficult moment, **b.)** A pessimist. No matter your answer, it's always best to do as directed. Thinking negative while isolating oneself doesn't add to the recovery. In Step 2, while inducing your thoughts about them, nothing has to be sad all the time. Engage in the possibility of a better tomorrow. It's your imagination. Make everything bright.

Finally, brothers and sisters, whatever is true, whatever is noble, whatever is right, whatever is pure, whatever is lovely, whatever is admirable—if anything is excellent or praiseworthy—think about such things

- Philippians 4:8

Now that you're single, exercise your liberty to partake in events or activities you neglected while in a relationship. Even more so, if your mate held you back from certain hobbies or "bucket list" entries, then now is the time to revisit your missions.

No matter where you are, there are at least 10-100 tourist attractions in most towns to explore and many are free. How so? Almost every city, no matter the size, has a tourist activities board. They are in charge of making sure the city can gain dollars from visitors and locals. From local fairs, doggy movie nights to light decorating ceremonies; all types of events are constructed to keep your attention.

Dance, party, read books, visit amusement parks; get active! Although you may still think about your ex, your stress will decrease and mind will settle. Laughter is a medicine. It calms your soul. Staying active benefits your mind and you won't be a victim of indulging in poisonous depression. Don't be afraid to search your phone for friends you haven't spoke to, they may have ideas as well.

As many of my clients can attest, while in a relationship, we directly or indirectly abandon our friends. Those people we spoke to almost everyday before the relationship, suddenly become strangers in our phones after. They're still your friends. They're still there. Call them. Friends have a habit of making us smile when we would rather not. This can also be a fantastic moment to create art.

Adele, an amazing British singer, wrote some of the most painfully accurate and legendary songs during heartbreak. She is powerful but her sorrow is what made the songs relative to people all across the world. No one gender, age or ethnicity could directly state, "This is made for us" solely because everyone hearing it felt like, "This was made for *me.*" Why not write a book, paint a portrait and create a play or song about what you're going through? If you love performing your craft, why not do so while enduring this journey? Maybe art isn't your gift but what about facing a fear?

Are you afraid of public speaking? Does the thought of owning your own home frighten you? Is the nightmare of not accomplishing a dream waking you at night? Whatever your fear is, challenge it with courage. As a boxer, I honestly feared sparring new people almost every time I stepped into the ring. I've boxed maybe 1,000 rounds. Right before a sparring match, my stomach would knot up, I would need air, water and sometimes prayer. This wasn't a championship match. This was just sparring. Amazingly, the act of confronting my fear was exhilarating. Why? It took my mind off of whoever occupied my thoughts.

Go out and have fun. In this day and age, there is a ton of websites dedicated to showcasing free, inexpensive or discounted events. We have unlimited excuses as to why we won't or can't follow this instruction. However, this fact outweighs them all: You can, you should and when you do, you may not remember why you fought this advice.

Why It Will Be Hard:

It feels more fun to wallow in isolation. That's why this is hard. Not to mention, it's also difficult to run from the thought of being a burden or killjoy to your friends. Nothing about getting over an ex will be easy. It's not supposed to be easy. If forgetting someone were so easy, we would cancel many cases of depression in our world. This will take time.

You can do your heart an injustice by indulging in nothingness. Sometimes that breaks your heart more than anything. Keeping yourself unhappy can cause a darkness to overwhelm you. From there, you can only harbor negative thoughts about life, your ex and even your future. The walls of your home, apartment or dorm suddenly resemble prison bars. A smile and happiness are now distant memories of things you formerly believed in but now see as fairytale. This isn't a beautiful reality at all.

The counterpunch for this mood is to fight it with subtle acts of joy. Watch a movie. Better yet, watch a movie you probably would never watch. For me, it's Romantic Comedies, affectionately known as, "Rom

Coms." When I was in a relationship, I would only watch these with a mate. After I was hurt, there wasn't a reason to watch them. Then I said, "Well, it couldn't hurt" and it didn't. They are some of the funniest and warmest movies written. For you, it may be action, suspense, horror or even fantasy. The overall goal is to battle your seemingly innate desire for sadness and challenge your mental status quo.

Bad Advice Many Follow:
"I just want to be alone. I feel better this way."

"The devil is a lie" is typically a response when someone discloses a statement that requires rebuking. The idea that being sad feels good is sick and poisonous. You are not better off sorrowful. You are only doing what your desperate mind feels most at ease with during this moment.

When you're alone, your mind can find all forms of evil and spirit breaking ideas to ponder. This is where violence, murder and even self-mutilation can seed. A future after committing any of the above is a dim future. As stated in previous text, there are many people who've killed others and themselves post-relationship. You don't want to add yourself to the list.

Just as you've never imagined being in this situation, you may never have seen yourself as a violent person. In times of despair and when we believe hope is lost, our primitive mind becomes a powerful authority. It's at this time that some believe caving into the perceived "easier behavior" is a default action. You think you have control.

Exclusion from people to learn more about yourself isn't the same as disappearing into the dead end tunnel of "Why me?" The difference? When exclusion is to build oneself, there is a level of positivity in this decision. The "Why me?" is associated with negativity and many times accompanied by doubt of self-worth.

The urge of isolation is strong and manipulative. While you may feel a sense of security from the problem at hand, you're indirectly chasing depression. It's in this phase that many don't escape. A friend of mine couldn't beat this moment for years. Their suicide attempts left permanent physical reminders of their voyage into the abyss of loneliness.

As I repeat, this won't be easy but all great moments in life require us to defeat ourselves. Your mind isn't always an ally in times like this. In reality, your mind may become a formidable enemy disguised as a guide. Who would imagine being faced with overcoming their own mind? No one imagines battling the seemingly unshakable sense to stay home and cry.

When standing toe to toe with the foe being yourself, it's a fight many rather not engage. This is what makes life worth living; the battles we don't expect but are expected to win. From here, how you deal with future relationships can be developed. By surpassing the immediate desire to flee into darkness, you show the light in yourself and circumstance. This chapter is not about accepting every invite and abandoning self-reflective moments. It's about enjoying your life and using happiness to overcome the adversity we call, desolation.

NOTES:

_____
_____
_____
_____
_____
_____
_____
_____
_____
_____
_____
_____
_____
_____
_____
_____
_____

Victory accompanies strength. Be strong…
Smile Again

www.GetOverThem.com

Step #9 Tomorrow Will Arrive

You WILL see your next birthday even if they're not present.

Why You Should:

Unless they fed you, housed you, made you, groomed you or many people call them, "God"...you will live without their existence. As a matter of fact, if they did all those things or their name was "God" you would still live. This is just another way self-inflicted wounds sabotage our minds. We waltz with our negative thoughts and emotions hoping to entice belief in a lie that's just that...a lie.

While you may find comfort basking in pity or despair, it's just a matter of time before you come to the realization, this person does not deserve your pain. This is one of many hurdles of life, but certainly not the end of it. You were something before they came into your life. Even if you believed they were your counterpart in a love story, just because they left doesn't mean you will cease to live "happily ever after".

The main reason behind believing there will be a tomorrow is solely based on the fact that you're currently living in a tomorrow or many tomorrows after your breakup. If tomorrow wasn't coming then it should not have come already. But it did, right? Now you have to live it. Have you thought about the good coming out of this ending?

It is over, yes but what good can breed from this cancellation of love? Really sit on that question. Is there a rainbow at the end of this story? If you can't see it, then create it. Only you can assemble the great work of art called, "My Love Life." This begins with the thought, "What good came out of this?" Despite being the victim or violator of your relationship's end, you are now the pilot of your heart's new destination. In order for you to fly into another place of happiness, you must first believe there will be another place and day to fly.

Once you've come to terms with answering, "What good came out of this?" the next portion is capitalizing on the good. Example: If the good is, "Now I can meet someone who will love me better." With the aforementioned, you can build on avoiding meeting people like your ex. What is most odd about relationships is we tend to forget the characteristics of our ex and just end up dating a new person who resembles the ex. This creates a cycle.

One reason you may not believe there is a tomorrow lies in your inability to accept the fact that the type of people you date may not benefit you. We date our parents, believe it or not. In many cases, even if we had unique bonds with our parents, we end up dating people who match their traits. Remember, your parents were the first man or woman you ever met. They are also the man or woman you've known longer than any other man or woman. This creates a wild reality many seldom research.

Your father may have been a good provider but a horrible person when it came to affection. He may have put food on the table, clothes on your back and a roof over your head but neglected to hug you, say, "I love you" and let you know how special you are to him. Your mother may have been so busy keeping the house together or being a businesswoman to the affect of missing out on your school or extra-curricular activities. When you think about your ex, what similarities do they have with your parent of the same sex? Are you chasing their love but not realizing their love was poisonous? Now you're dating someone who can't love you the way you want to be loved because they love you the way you're accustomed to being loved…incorrectly.

When you're constantly dating the wrong person, your tomorrow seems bleak for many points. **1.)** The next person will not be an improvement and you are actually looking to date someone similar because that's your, "type." **2.)** You know your behavior is unjust and childish but you refuse to change. No matter the point, it's crucial you look inward to locate why you believe your future won't be bright. Have you looked deeper into you? Do you love you?

That's a scary question to most but a very important question. As stated in Chapter 10: Countdown #1, knowing yourself is powerful but loving yourself is a journey some never dare to actually embark upon. Loving yourself demands a pre-requisite of willingness to love ugliness.

We all aren't the best brothers, sisters, fathers, mothers, lovers, daughters or sons. It's impossible to be perfect all the time, but we can do our best to be our best. We can look in the mirror and love our effort at life. We can look in the mirror and love the fact we're not giving up on our dreams. We can look in the mirror and love our reflection no matter the tint, weight or scars. Loving yourself is a task fit for royalty.

This creates an inner joy, which has permanent residence no matter the situation. If someone calls me ugly, I'm almost appalled by their statement and ignorance. I look in the mirror and see a handsome, good and ambitious man of God. That's what I see. Ugly? Sorry, I'm unfamiliar with the person you're aiming to injure with your words. Why? I love me. It wasn't easy but it occurred.

While in middle school, I actually was popular and had many girlfriends. When high school began, puberty took over what was once a boyish hairless face. The pimples made me a stage 5 "pizza face." Calling me an acne monster would be accurate but it wouldn't make me believe I'm any worse looking than say, Brad Pitt.

For some reason, I lied to myself and believed I was the coolest thing since wearing bell-bottoms in the 70's or carrying a boombox on your shoulder in the 90's. It was my truth. This was my armor. Looking at those pimples and denying the desire to say, "You're ugly like everyone says" was a daily battle but it was done. You can win too.

Believe there is a tomorrow. Believe it because it is already here. You are attractive, goal oriented, special and worthy to be loved. This is your test and will bring about your testimony. In no time, you will be in love again and yesterday's sorrow will only exist in yesterday.

Why It Will Be Hard:

Honestly, it feels good. It feels good to be sad and believe life is no more because one person is no longer in it. It's an odd feeling but it does give us a false feeling of satisfaction. It's a lie, nonetheless. Don't trust its easiness.

I've written about my friend suffering from depression and suicidal thoughts, which led to multiple attempts. They are proof of the unreliability of that feeling. Also, attacking the aftereffects of a breakup with, "My tomorrow will be brighter" isn't an immediate thought. If we do utter such a phrase, it's a half-hearted attempt at making a sad situation sound better. In reality, it's okay to say, "This is hard and it hurts **but it will get better**."

Unless you dated the person for literally a week or barely knew their last name, it will be hard. I once had a "girlfriend" in middle school. Her name was Antoya. We dated for about…six days. I don't remember feeling sad or damaged by that conclusion. If they meant something to you, you're supposed to endure a little pain. The hard part is believing there will be a tomorrow. The easy part is believing there won't be.

You owe it to yourself to have your moment of tearfulness and remembrance of your past circumstance. Just keep in mind that when you are done crying and wishing they were there or you never dated them in the first place, you also keep in mind that each second you breathe is one more moment inching closer to another tomorrow.

Bad Advice Many Follow:

"This pain will keep getting harder to bear. There is no silver lining."

There was a hilarious picture on the Internet. The photo was of a bed but just the box spring edge. The edge was made of all rusted steel. Now, what made this funny was the universal truth those sharing it owned. *We all have hit our leg on that edge.*

While some of us laughed conservatively, others may have giggled so hard, they cried tears of happiness. This nostalgic photo should have won an award for most relatable photo of all time. Now, we all laugh today but when your ankle or shin collided with that edge, you couldn't imagine laughing.

During this time, you may have shouted, screamed, cried or even fell to the ground in sheer agony. You knew this excruciating moment wasn't comedic. As you lay there holding whatever body part, you hoped the more you cried, the more you healed. Even still, your mind went into, "This will never be over" mode.

You just hit that edge, figuratively. You are in that mode but amazingly, you may find yourself laughing at this very moment later on. No, you may not ever find this as a photo online but in your mind, the very thought of you crying over this person may be worth a smirk or two.

Don't listen to yourself or anyone else give you the, "You'll never find another like them" or "You should have known better" speech. If you're hurt, guilt won't encourage you. There will be another day that you may even run into another bed frame edge. With whatever occurs, tomorrow has no choice but to arrive. Also, tomorrow brings with it more chances to laugh at these moments of your life.

NOTES:

_____

_____

_____

_____

_____

_____

_____

_____

_____

_____

_____

_____

_____

_____

_____

_____

You will be loved again...
Smile Again

www.GetOverThem.com

Step # 10: Pray/Meditate*

Sometimes in moments like this, we forget the power of prayer.

*For Atheists and Agnostics, you will find guidance after the, ***"Bad Advice Many Follow"*** subchapter. *

Why You Should:

Prayer is a powerful and the best tool in our arsenal for handling break ups. We all have choices to make in our daily lives but the choice of going to a quiet place and giving your burdens to God is something many neglect to do.

When it comes to prayer, it's amazingly important to find a place where you can be alone in thought. There is a certain power with praying alongside others but there lies a beautiful somberness when you can pray for yourself. Your prayer won't always sound as smooth as the priest or pastor but you can manage. Praying in isolation isn't my advice; it's in the Holy Bible.

But when you pray, go into your room, close the door and pray to your Father, who is unseen. Then your Father, who sees what is done in secret, will reward you.
Matthew 6:6

Honestly, from my perspective, praying about your issue in front of others may bring more attention to your trouble than direction or support. They may not pray for you or pray for what you're ready to receive. Example: They're praying that you find someone new and better, while you're praying to stop abusing the drugs you're using to ease your suffering. At the time, you may fear being judged by your peers about disclosing your habit. To add, the Holy Bible breaks down another scripture:

"When you pray, you are not to be like the hypocrites; for they love to stand and pray in the synagogues and on the street corners so that they may be seen by men. Truly I say to you, they have their reward in full
-Matthew 6:5

This isn't to discourage peer assistance but to clarify the need of an intimate connection between you and God. Remember, everyone isn't an advisor or great for every occasion. Some of your friends may not know how to deal with this traumatic moment. This is why we go to God. This is why we pray. Give your burdens to Him. It's too hard to just believe you'll figure it out on your own.

28 "Come to me, all you who are weary and burdened, and I will give you rest. 29 Take my yoke upon you and learn from me, for I am gentle and humble in heart, and you will find rest for your souls. 30 For my yoke is easy and my burden is light."

- Matthew 11:28-30

Prayer, in any religion, is about trusting your cares on a higher authority. Trust, this five-letter word is huge while you circumvent the confusing voyage of rediscovering your happiness and wholeness. During this period, trusting yourself to make good decisions may be a horrible idea.

As stated before, many people use drugs and some plot their suicide or even the kidnapping or murder of their former mate. Some even reconsider the pain their ex inflicted and use, "Since I've been with them for so long, I should just stay with them. I don't want to be lonely or start back over with someone new." Trusting your emotional or illogical decision-making isn't a risk you want to take. Trust God.

Trust in the LORD with all your heart, and do not lean on your own understanding.

Proverbs 3:5

It is better to take refuge in the LORD than to trust in man.
- Psalms 118:8

Prayer also brings about forgiveness. What power forgiveness is! Many times we think forgiveness is about the other person. No, forgiveness is about you. When you forgive yourself or the person for what they've done to you, it opens an opportunity for you to breathe. When you're being tormented by someone's actions or the guilt of your own, what provides comfort for your distress? Forgiveness.

Forgiveness just says, "I'm no longer allowing this burden to cause me stress." That's it. You're not saying," I forgive you. Please hurt me again." Nor are you saying, "I forgive myself and won't feel the affects of my actions." All you're saying is, "This isn't going to weigh me down, anymore." That's the power of forgiveness. It places the authority of your happiness back in your hands. You don't have to wait on your ex to apologize or to see some drastic change in your life. You can pray and ask God for forgiveness of your actions or your ex's and move on to another chapter in your life.

And when you stand praying, if you hold anything against anyone, forgive them, so that your Father in heaven may forgive you your sins."
-Mark 11:25

One of the most powerful prayers you can pray is, "Please, heavenly Father, don't allow this tragedy to alter my heart. Let me love the way I love and believe I can be loved the way I truly deserve." Why is the aforementioned prayer, "powerful"? You're asking God, "Please don't let this change me." Many people are what we call, "hard lovers." I'm happily guilty of being a person who loves hard.

A person who loves hard doesn't love sparingly. We give our all with no strings attached. When your heart is broken, it is at many times difficult to fight the feeling of, "Maybe I shouldn't be so nice" or "Maybe I do give too much." No, you are false. You are never too nice. You are never too much of a giver. What you are missing is a person who is just as nice or as much of a giver. If you dated someone who reciprocated your characteristics, then this thought wouldn't exist. Pray you stay who you are despite what was done to you. I actually wrote an "interesting" story about this.

Batman, Spiderman and Superman were sitting in a bar. Now 11 years into their retirement, they open up to one another. Batman asks Spiderman, "Why do you fight crime?" Spiderman replies, "I was stung by a radioactive spider which gave me super strength, speed and agility. After watching my uncle die at the hands of a thug, I decided to help others from living the pain of what I endured."

Spiderman asks Batman, "Why do you fight crime?" Batman says, "When I lost my parents at the hands of a thug, I decided no one needed to experience the pain I endured. I worked out, learned martial arts and began to make a difference in my community." Superman saw both super heroes looking at him. He knew the question and began to answer.

"I fight crime because I saw something wrong and decided to fix it. I'm not from this planet, so I can't claim a thug killed my parents. However, my entire planet was destroyed because of horrible actions of those around me. Just like my home, this world is filled with turmoil and evil people, I just want to do whatever I can to level the playing field." Batman and Spiderman nodded in agreement. Then a nosey elderly lady, who eavesdropped on their conversation, asked them all a question.

"You all could have not been super heroes. Instead you could have sold your talents or just did nothing. Every single day you put your life on the line for people who barely thank you. You fight for the broken, poor and rich but seldom receive the appreciation you deserve. Did you ever just think, "Why should I fight for them?"

Superman responded, "Yes, I believe we all second -guessed ourselves at least once, (Batman and Spiderman both nod in agreement) but I can't stop being myself. God made me this way. There are days I neglect to pray. There are times when I don't care to acknowledge the blessings He gave me. However, I was created in His image. With that said, I have fun serving as He directed. It's not stressful to be who God made me to be and " She interrupts, "But you're not from Earth. How can you believe in a higher being?"

"Even though I'm not from this planet, the Holy Bible says in Genesis 1:1, 'In the beginning God created the heavens and the earth.' Heaven is plural. Maybe that's where my people are from; one of the heavens. Either way, I sacrifice and serve because that's what brings me joy.

Being a child of God, to me, means being a servant. Allowing horrible people or circumstances to detract from what makes me who I am won't bring me joy."

What brings you joy? Are you second-guessing your goodness because of this breakup? Are you in the process of believing, "Maybe the way I am isn't good enough"? Unless you knowingly did something wrong, why harbor belief that being good is a bad thing? Don't torture yourself for being what the world should be. If you were the violator in the relationship, you can improve.

Perfection is meant for death, in my opinion. How can you be perfect and sinless on earth? No one can live without sinning. It's just too easy to sin and many times we commit acts of sin unconsciously. What I want you to see is we all fall short of grace. If you've cheated, lied or betrayed your mate, you can look introspectively and do better. Pray to improve, and then start improving. Don't waste a prayer by just praying and waiting for God to do something. Pray then starting working on your error. Otherwise your prayer is in vain.

14 What good is it, my brothers, if someone says he has faith but does not have works? Can that faith save him? **15** If a brother or sister is poorly clothed and lacking in daily food, **16** and one of you says to them, "Go in peace, be warmed and filled," without giving them the things needed for the body, what good is that? **17** So also faith by itself, if it does not have works, is dead.

James 2:14-17

God is there. Ask for comfort, happiness, strength and resilience. Prayer is a power and God is safety. Keep close to whatever religious doctrine you follow. From there you can gain the courage and bravado needed to see another day and eventually get over your ex.

Why This Is Hard:

It's easy to ask, "Where was God?" after you're broken. The real question should be, "Was God always intertwined in this relationship? Did you invite God into your relationship? Did you pray for your mate's wellbeing on a regular basis? Did they pray for you? Did you two pray together? Many people can't answer, "Yes" to all or any of these previous questions. Therein lies the issue.

This isn't about Islam, Christianity or any particular faith. This is about being consistent to your faith. It's amazing how we fail to bring God into our love but expect Him to be there when it's over. Although He will be there, it creates a wonderful question, "Why did it take pain for you to seek Him?" For some, this is hitting the mark.

We feel a sense of abandonment when things go wrong. Especially if we're good people, as most are. When you fall, you wonder why would God allow you to fall? Even I dislike this phrase, "Maybe it was for your own good."

This is easier to believe if God gave you warning signs. In some cases, He gave far too many and for others, the relationship ended so abruptly that no signs may have been seen. For those blessed and cursed to see the signs, did you acknowledge them or ignore them?

Praying to God for healing after knowingly going against His instruction is sometimes impossible. You feel embarrassed for hoping your eyes lied after the truth you witnessed. Kneeling and asking for help from Someone you may have left behind is a humbling experience but it's necessary. Think about it, if God was only for people who did the right things…who would pray to Him?

The act of praying every night doesn't automatically make it easier to continue this habit after a breakup. For those who are prayer warriors, a breakup can still be hard to deal with. Your faith is challenged and the mere idea of asking God questions may be the last thing on your list. No matter what you are in terms of your faith or consistency of prayer, you have power in prayer. It may not be easy but if you challenge yourself to do so in the face of shame or pain, victory will be your result.

Bad Advice Many Follow:
"God wasn't there when I got hurt. Why will He show up now?"

The best enemy is one who knows their foe better than they know themselves. In this case, your heart is the foe and your mind is the enemy. This is an age-old battle between the two. If you haven't noticed, your mind is supposed to always be the victor. However, your mind is typically the loser on many occasions. Don't trust your heart in this matter.

> *The heart is deceitful above all things and beyond cure. Who can understand it?*
> *Jeremiah 17:9*

Your heart isn't to be trusted in times of excruciating turmoil. Without a shadow of a doubt, most of your poor decision-making will come from your heart. The only reason you laugh at your past actions is because only then when you're numb to your injury do you see the naivety in your behavior.

I once called a girlfriend 30+ times a day with no answer. 30+ times! A wise man would have realized, "She is with her new guy. Take the hint." No matter how many hints I received that she may be untrustworthy, I closed my eyes to them all. So what did I do? Kept calling. She would randomly pick up, give some bogus excuse, rush me off the phone and the next day I would go right back to calling. Almost a decade later, the pain no longer exists, I can laugh at myself and even give advice to my younger self. That was an act of my heart.

There is nothing more disgusting than feeling single while in a relationship. My heart didn't want to feel this way. Instead of giving the torch to my mind, the heart overwhelmed my logic and I kept calling. Right now I'm giggling at my younger self walking in circles around my neighborhood saying, "I'm only going to call another 5 times." How did I make calling 30+ times logical? I didn't, but now reliving this moment reinvigorates a thought.

Thinking back, I actually don't want to laugh at the younger me, I empathize with that part of me now. Our hearts are actually beautiful. The heart wants to believe the best in everyone. The heart wants to believe in happily ever after. The heart wants to smile everyday and not have any sad days. That's the heart. The heart also, when broken, wants to languish alone far from anyone who can heal it, even God.

Looking back, this period in my life was filled with veiled joy. Much like anyone aimlessly floating through the river of grief called a breakup, we put on a smile for everyone yet own no real estate in Happiness. Subtly, we begin to find our footing in faith. Ironically, it is the heart that wants to find comfort in God. Your mind may have initiated the action but your heart enforces the follow through. Why? Because it wants to be loved. It wants to be healed. A heart just wants to be happy and whole.

Our lives are inundated with a series of choices. Some are as simple as "What to wear?" while others consist of delicate answers such as, "What is my five year plan?" No matter the decision, you have to make it. This is one of the many cons of being an adult. You and only you are in charge of making tough choices regarding your future.

This choice can be the easiest you'll ever make or the most complicated. The worst advice you can ever follow is, "Prayer won't change anything." Why is that advice so horrible? It's horrible because of its truth. Praying and not taking immediate action on your prayer, as stated above, is a waste of prayer.

After you pray, begin reading books about overcoming heartache. If you're not much of a reader, watch comedies and laugh. Go online or call friends to find out events in town. Get yourself away from yourself. See a new play, go bowling or write a funny story about your most embarrassing moment but don't *just* pray.

For Atheists/Agnostic

Meditate. Think inwardly. Find the inner voice, peace or direction needed to help you during this trial. There will be triumph. You may find an answer within yourself to boost your morale and give you direction. Take the time alone to be with yourself. No distractions. No technology. Just you and your bareness. Concentrate on nothingness. Then, once your mind is clear, only think about peaceful ways to get to happiness. This is your task. You hold the key.

NOTES:

This book is the beginning...
Smile Again

www.GetOverThem.com

The End:

My tears are old. My pain is old. My burden is no more. However, my memory is intact. Empathizing with you outweighs the idea of sympathizing. Empathy proves I can actually understand where you're coming from because I've been there. Sympathy proves I can say, "It's going to get better."

Road trip; that's what this journey will be called. You are going on a road trip in your life. Sometimes it will rain and slow everyone down. Other times the sky will clear and you may find the drive more pleasant. Whatever you do, keep driving. If getting over an ex was simple, no one would call it a heartbreak.

The reason why this should be taken seriously is because you are worth the effort. This isn't about your ex or anyone else but you. Without you being whole and happy, the world may miss out on the next Adele, Whitney Houston, Denzel Washington, Ricky Martin, Miguel Cotto, Babe Ruth, Aziz Ansari, Trevor Noah or Jon Stewart. You may hold the next world changing invention in your head. If you gloss over this bump in the road, you may never recover from the accident.

We need you whole. Your family and friends need you whole. Most importantly, you need you whole. We need the version of you who loves wholeheartedly. We need the version of you that you are longing to reconnect with. There isn't a better reason to get over your ex than this, "When you're finally over them, how awesome would it be to laugh at how ugly you've cried?"

One day that line may make you chuckle. One day your sadness will be past tense. One day you may write me a message stating, "I got over them." One day you will smile again. Whenever those days arrive, they will be met with joy and you will be over your ex…FOR GOOD.

About The Author

Despite losing his mother at 12, having his father abandon him the same day and being classified as an orphan, Egypt may have been knocked down, but never knocked out.

Over a span of 10 years, Egypt has led a life many consider a fairytale. His work in Black history storytelling, relationship counseling and HIV education opened doors many seldom see. He's appeared on MTV, BET, Apollo Theater, FOX with Lee Pitts, in addition to countless radio shows, magazine and performance appearances.

Egypt has shared stages with A-list celebrities such as John Legend, Alicia Keys and Magic Johnson. He adopted the name "Egypt" because he plans to influence the world just as the great African empire has influenced the earth.

He's touched stages in Johannesburg, South Africa, Doha Qatar, Barbados, Haiti, Trinidad and Tobago and a **TEDx** Talk in Amman, Jordan. Not to neglect he's gained two degrees while being on the Dean's list, graduated Phi Theta Kappa Honors, won the Florida State PAL Boxing Championship, is a devout Christian, created the AIDS Awareness Poets Inc. and the AIDS Games.

He wrote three top selling relationship books, "How Good Is Sex?" "Change Him… In 100 pages" and "Love Is Not An STD". He is also the youngest (27) "Alumni of the Year" award recipient at Palm Beach State College for his work in HIV/AIDS. Yet, his highest achievement occurred April 6th, 2014 by marrying his dream woman.

He is proof, that no matter how your life starts, you can change the middle and alter the ending. His story has inspired many and continues to be a reason why some believe their yesterday won't dictate their tomorrow because they've made a decision to live right…today.

For Booking/Workshop Inquires:

Email: ICan@GetOverThem.com

Website: www.GetOverThem.com

For More Work By "Egypt" Visit www.WebsiteOfEgypt.com

Acknowledgements

To my wife: Thank you for saying, "I do." You've helped make me a better man.

To my sister, Chasity Walker: I love you and thank you for your sacrifice.

To Mrs. Marion Williams: Thank you for bringing my history to me.

To my little sister, Chukia Williams: I love you. Be the mom you know you can be.

To my niece, Diamond Bynes: I love you and don't entertain garbage men.

To my nephew, Kenrick Thomas Jr. Aka "Lil X": I love you. Be better than me.

To my Dad: Thanks for my amazing story. Your absence made me a man.

To my Uncle Tom: I love you for being the man I wish to be.

To the Ruffins, Pop and Mom: I thank God for giving me another set of parents.

To Arthur Wylie: Thanks for being an amazing addition to my family.

To Omar Tyree: Thanks for being an inspiration to me and authors everywhere.

To the Houston Family: Thanks for making me part of your family. I will be loyal.

To Kemet and Deedee: You're precious to me…even though you're dogs.

To the Rodriguez Family: Thank you for teaching me determination.

To the Hernandez Family: Thank you for showing me family.

To the Stitt family: Thank you for showing me faith.

To Marielle Michel: Thank you for supporting me before I was me.

To Sevown Matthews: Thank you for giving me a place to stay.

To Ancel Pratt III: Thank you for being the leader I needed to see.

To Ms. Robinson: Thank you for helping inspire my love for HIV education.

To Jasmin McNeil: Thank you for crying when you saw me on BET. Inspiration.

To Adrian Sutton: Thank you for indirectly encouraging me to be me.

To Duane Boucard: Thank you for not forgetting what friendship is.

To Brian Poem: Thank you for being my road buddy.

To Noel Stitt: Thank you for being the best friend money could buy, ha!

To Francisco Hernandez: Thanks for being the best friend cash can't buy, ha!

To Mable Dell Robinson: Mother, I love you. And thank you for Chas.

To Venise and Gloria: Thank you for being the first to believe in me.

To Irone Singleton: Thank you for being the example I needed to see.

To UNC, Thank you for inspiring me to be more diverse.

To all of my supporters: Thank you for never giving up on my dreams. Without you, I would be a man writing a letter to himself. You believe in my work and are the breath I breathe.

www.ingramcontent.com/pod-product-compliance
Lightning Source LLC
Chambersburg PA
CBHW032042090426
42744CB00004B/93